SYLVIA BARBARA SOBERTON

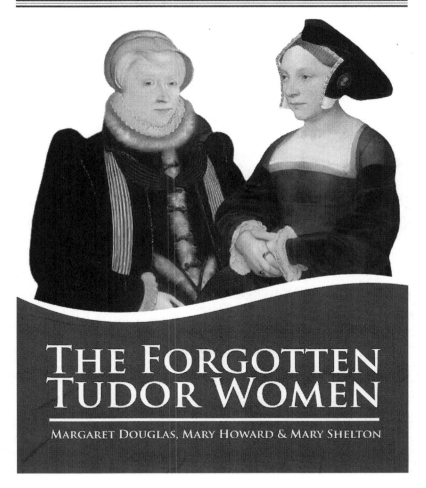

THE FORGOTTEN TUDOR WOMEN

MARGARET DOUGLAS, MARY HOWARD & MARY SHELTON

THE FORGOTTEN TUDOR WOMEN

MARGARET DOUGLAS, MARY HOWARD & MARY SHELTON

Facebook page:

www.facebook.com/theforgottentudorwomen

Editorial services: Jenny Toney Quinlan

ISBN-13: 978-1507764985

ISBN-10: 1507764987

Contents

INTRODUCTION

Everyone knows that Henry VIII had six wives, two sisters and two daughters. All of these women received attention in academic circles and are subjects of countless biographies. Not many people, however, realize that Henry VIII also had a niece, a daughter-in-law and a mistress, who were close friends. These women were Margaret Douglas, Mary Howard and Mary Shelton, and this book examines their lives.

Margaret Douglas was Henry VIII's niece and incurred her uncle's wrath twice when she fell in love with men of her own choosing. Charismatic, beautiful and cunning, Margaret found herself imprisoned in the Tower of London on three occasions, and each time, as she admitted, "not for matters of treason, but for matters of love". Mary Howard was Anne Boleyn's first cousin and protégée and married the King's illegitimate son, Henry Fitzroy. After his death, she was penniless, as Henry VIII refused to grant her rights to her jointure. Spirited, intelligent and "too wise for a woman", Mary made her way through the Tudor court by sheer force of determination. Mary Shelton, another first cousin of Anne Boleyn, became Henry VIII's mistress for a brief spell, but she had apparently captivated the King, as

1

there were rumours that he would take her as his fourth wife. She was something of a trailblazer, one of the first women who not only transcribed but also wrote poetry and held pro-feminist views on women in an age when daughters, sisters and cousins were treated as chattel and used for the advancement of men.

These three women are best known for contributing to the *Devonshire Manuscript,* a courtly anthology that has survived to the present day. The poems in this extraordinary manuscript contain themes of love and loss and evoke the backstabbing environment of the Tudor court. The lives of Margaret Douglas, Mary Howard and Mary Shelton were more colourful that any soap opera, and it is a high time to tell their stories and reclaim them from obscurity.

Glossary of names

The Howards:

Mary Howard, Duchess of Richmond: Daughter of Thomas Howard, 3rd Duke of Norfolk. Married Henry Fitzroy, Duke of Richmond, on 26 November 1533.

Widowed in 1536, she struggled to obtain jointure from Henry VIII.

Thomas Howard, 2nd Duke of Norfolk: Mary's grandfather. He married twice, first to Elizabeth Tilney and after her death to her cousin, Agnes Tilney. Both marriages produced several children.

Agnes Howard, née Tilney, Dowager Duchess of Norfolk: Mary's grandmother, who was styled the Dowager Duchess of Norfolk after her husband's death in 1524. She ran a household for young noblewomen and attended court on occasion. She was the mother of Lord Thomas Howard, who fell in love with Margaret Douglas.

Thomas Howard, Earl of Surrey, and from 1524, 3rd Duke of Norfolk: Mary's father and the leading peer of Henry VIII's court. Courtier, soldier and diplomat, he was at the centre of Tudor politics right up until his arrest in 1546. He was the eldest son of Thomas Howard, 2nd Duke of Norfolk and his first wife, Elizabeth Tilney. He married twice: in 1495 to Anne of York, sister-in-law to Henry VII, and on her death in November 1511, he married Elizabeth Stafford.

Elizabeth Howard née Stafford, Duchess of Norfolk: Mary's mother. She was the daughter of Edward

Stafford, 3rd Duke of Buckingham, who was executed in 1521. Thomas Howard separated from her in 1534, throwing her out of their household at Kenninghall.

Henry Howard, Earl of Surrey: Mary's elder brother and a renowned Tudor poet, courtier and soldier. Married to Frances, daughter of John de Vere, 15th Earl of Oxford. Executed on false charges of high treason on 19 January 1547.

Frances Howard, née de Vere, Countess of Surrey: Henry Howard's wife and mother of his children.

Thomas Howard, 1st Viscount Howard of Bindon: Mary's younger brother.

Lord Thomas Howard: Son of Thomas Howard, 2nd Duke of Norfolk and Agnes Tilney, and Mary's half uncle Condemned for treason after secretly marrying Henry VIII's niece, Margaret Douglas. Died of a fever in the Tower of London on 31 October 1537.

Thomas Howard, 4th Duke of Norfolk: The eldest son and heir of Henry Howard, Earl of Surrey, and Frances de Vere. Raised in Mary Howard's household after his father's execution. Inherited the dukedom of Norfolk on his grandfather's death in 1554. His plans to marry Mary, Queen of Scots, sent him to the executioner's block in 1572.

Elizabeth 'Bess' Reppes, née Holland: Mistress of Thomas Howard, 3rd Duke of Norfolk, and Mary Howard's friend. She testified against her lover and was rewarded with jewellery for her compliance. She married shortly after her lover's arrest and died in childbed in 1548.

The Sheltons

Mary Shelton: Daughter of John and Anne Shelton, mistress of Henry VIII and a poet. Romantically linked to Henry Norris and Francis Weston, men executed in 1536 as alleged lovers of Queen Anne Boleyn. By 1546 she married Anthony Heveningham and bore him several children. She remarried to Philip Appleyard at an unknown date and died in 1571.

Anne Shelton, née Boleyn: Mary's mother and governess in the joint household of Princess Elizabeth and Lady Mary. Sister of Thomas Boleyn and aunt of Queen Anne. Died in 1556.

John Shelton: Mary's father and a steward in the joint household of Princess Elizabeth and Lady Mary.

John Shelton the younger: Mary's brother and the eldest son and heir of John Shelton. Married Margaret Parker, the sister of Jane, Viscountess of Rochford. Their daughter, Mary Shelton Scudamore, was one of the most prominent ladies in Queen Elizabeth's Privy Chamber.

Thomas Shelton: One of Mary's brothers, who served as a groom porter in the Tower of London.

Gabrielle Shelton: One of Mary's sisters. She was recorded as a nun of Barking and living in Carrow Priory near Norwich in 1536.

The Douglas-Stuart line:

Margaret Douglas, Countess of Lennox: Daughter of Margaret Tudor, eldest daughter of Henry VII and widow of James IV of Scotland, and Archibald Douglas, Earl of Angus, Margaret Tudor's second husband. Margaret was the first cousin of Tudor queens Mary and Elizabeth and the aunt of Mary Stuart, Queen of Scots.

Margaret Tudor, Queen of Scotland: Margaret Douglas's mother, widow of James IV and second wife of Archibald Douglas. After their secret marriage in 1514, she lost the title of regent and was forced to escape to England, where she gave birth to Margaret. After separation with Archibald in 1518, she had no other contact with her daughter other than through letters. Her third husband was Henry Stuart, Lord Methven. She died intestate in 1541 and desired that her jewels be given to Margaret Douglas.

James V of Scotland: Son of Margaret Tudor and James IV, and Margaret Douglas's half brother. He married the French Mary of Guise as his second wife in 1538. The couple had several children, including sons, but only Mary, the future Queen of Scots, survived to adulthood.

Matthew Stuart, 4th Earl of Lennox: Margaret Douglas's husband and father of her eight children. He married Margaret at St James's Palace on 29 June 1544. They had a happy marriage, as several of their still-extant letters affirm; Matthew called Margaret "his good Meg" or "sweet Madge".

Henry Stuart, Lord Darnley: The oldest surviving son of Margaret Douglas and Matthew Stuart. He married Mary, Queen of Scots, in 1565 and fathered a child with her, the future King James VI of Scotland. Darnley was murdered on 10 February 1567.

Mary Stuart, Queen of Scots: She was born on 8 December 1542 in Linlithgow Palace, West Lothian, Scotland. She was the only surviving child of James V of Scotland and his second wife, Mary of Guise. Her father died when Mary was only six days old, making her Mary, Queen of Scots. She spent most of her childhood in France while Scotland was ruled by regents, and in 1558, she married the Dauphin of France, Francis, who ascended the French throne as King Francis II in 1559. Mary briefly became Queen consort of France, until Francis II's death in 1560. Widowed, Mary returned to Scotland, and four years later she married her first cousin, Henry Stuart, Lord Darnley. She was thus Margaret Douglas's niece and daughter-in-law.

Charles Stuart, 5th Earl of Lennox: The second surviving child of Margaret Douglas and Matthew Stuart. His secret marriage to Elizabeth Cavendish, arranged by Margaret Douglas and Elizabeth's mother, Bess of Hardwick, displeased Queen Elizabeth and sent his mother to the Tower of London for the third time. He died at the age of twenty-one in 1576.

Arbella Stuart: Daughter of Charles Stuart and Elizabeth Cavendish, and Margaret Douglas's granddaughter.

James VI and I: Born on 19 June 1566, James was the son of Mary, Queen of Scots, and Henry Stuart, Lord Darnley. He became King of Scotland as James VI from 24 July 1567 and King of England and Ireland as James I from the union of the Scottish and English crowns on 24 March 1603 until his death. The kingdoms of Scotland and England were individual sovereign states, with their own parliaments, judiciary and law systems, though both were ruled by James in personal union.

CHAPTER 1:
PRINCESS OF SCOTLAND

The circumstances of Margaret Douglas's birth were turbulent to say the least. Her mother, Margaret Tudor, who married King James IV of Scotland in 1503, became a widow after James was killed during the disastrous battle of Flodden in 1513. Appointed as regent for her small son, James V, Queen Margaret fell passionately in love with Archibald Douglas, Earl of Angus, and married him on 14 August 1514. By this hasty marriage, she lost the regency of Scotland and found herself in a difficult position.

The only solution at the time was to flee to the court of Margaret's brother, Henry VIII. Dragged away from the safety of her home and travelling in an advanced state of pregnancy, Queen Margaret was seized with labour pains and forced to seek shelter in the Harbottle Castle owned by Thomas, Lord Dacre. She could hardly have observed the standard ritual of "taking her chamber" normally required of an expectant mother, and her labour proved to be very difficult. On 8 October 1515, the Queen Dowager "was delivered and brought to bed of a fair young lady".[1] The immediate baptism of the child under the name of Margaret

Douglas was hastily arranged and, as Lord Dacre recorded, "with such convenience as could or might be had in this barren and wild district".[2]

Although Margaret Douglas was born prematurely, she was in perfect health and thriving, but her mother was very ill after the delivery. The Queen Dowager later recalled that the fear and jeopardy she was in at the time caused her to be "delivered of a child fourteen days afore my time to my great spoil and extreme danger".[3] She had no more children after this prolonged labour.

As soon as she recovered from her "intolerable pain" and the fear for her life had passed, Queen Margaret and her infant daughter arrived in England.[4] The baby girl was treated as a princess and placed in the royal nursery, where she joined Henry VIII's daughter, Princess Mary, born in February 1516. By June 1517, the Queen Dowager and her child were back in Scotland and reunited with Margaret Douglas's father, Archibald.

The relationship of Margaret's parents can only be described with one word: volatile. During one of their notorious quarrels, when Margaret Douglas was only three years old, Archibald snatched her from her mother's arms and placed her in the fortress of Tantallon in

Haddingtonshire, where she was provided with a household of her own. Because Queen Margaret sought a divorce from Archibald Douglas, he did not allow her to see their daughter. Many people, including Henry VIII's wife, Katherine of Aragon, tried to convince Queen Margaret that by divorcing Archibald, she would disinherit her own daughter. Queen Margaret was convinced, however, that she had married Archibald in good faith, and thus the legitimacy of Margaret Douglas could not legally suffer.

Margaret's childhood was scarred by the discord between her parents. Separated from her mother, Margaret was constantly on the move, accompanying her father wherever he went. By 1530, the safest place for Margaret was England, and so she moved to the court of her uncle Henry VIII, where she was placed in the household of his daughter, Mary; the girls were only four months apart in age and formed a lifelong friendship that would survive until Mary's death in 1558.

Margaret and Mary were old enough to understand and discuss the political situation in England and form their own conclusions. It was probably from Princess Mary's point of view that Margaret learned about Henry VIII's mistress and queen-to-be, Anne Boleyn. Margaret's closest female relatives in England, Princess Mary and her aunt,

Mary Tudor Brandon, were both hostile towards Anne Boleyn and bore her small love. It is possible that Margaret shared their opinion about Henry VIII's beloved one, but if she did, she was careful enough not to voice her opinions publicly.

The first glimpse of Margaret Douglas in the royal accounts dates to 6 April 1530, when she received grants of clothing from the King. She was presented with three new gowns, kirtles and matching sleeves. On 14 December 1530, she received a magnificent gown of crimson velvet lined with cloth of gold with a matching kirtle of crimson velvet and sleeves of black velvet. Other gifts included an extravagant nightgown lined with fur, a cloak of black cloth and two expensive French hoods.[5] From these recorded provisions, we learn that Margaret was served by two ladies-in-waiting at the time, as they were also provided with items of clothing.[6] During the Christmas festivities of 1530, Margaret Douglas and Princess Mary received a gift of money from Henry VIII "to disport with all this Christmas".[7]

While Margaret and Mary celebrated together at Beaulieu Palace, the atmosphere at court was grim. That Christmas marked Katherine of Aragon's "great triumph" as she was celebrating her victory at the Blackfriars trial, where she crushed the King's hopes for a quick divorce.[8] Never one to give up, the Queen was not only fighting for preservation of her own dignity but also defending her daughter's right to the throne. At this point, Katherine of Aragon believed that if she resisted, Henry VIII would finally realize his mistake and repudiate Anne Boleyn, something that Anne feared the most. Little did anyone know that in due course Henry VIII would take matters into his own hands. Although she could not know it at the time, this new and inevitable course of action would also change Margaret's own life.

NOTES

[1] Strickland, *Lives of the Queens of Scotland and English Princesses,* Volume 2, p. 273.
[2] Ibid., p. 274.
[3] Perry, *Sisters to the King,* p. 180.
[4] Ibid., p. 179.
[5] Hayward, *Dress at the Court of Henry VIII,* pp. 202-3.
[6] Ibid.
[7] Harris, *Privy Purse Expenses of Henry VIII,* p. 98.
[8] Ives, *The Life and Death of Anne Boleyn,* p. 128.

CHAPTER 2:
A COURTIER'S DAUGHTER

Mary Howard was born on an unknown date in 1519 as one of the five children born to Thomas Howard and his second wife, Elizabeth Stafford. Mary's great-grandfather was John, Lord Howard, who was created the first Howard Duke of Norfolk in 1483, when the last remaining member of the Mowbray family, who previously held this title, died. John's son Thomas received the earldom of Surrey, and it became family tradition for the Duke of Norfolk's son to claim the title of Earl of Surrey. John Howard was slain beside King Richard III at the battle of Bosworth in 1485 and, although his dukedom should have passed on to his son, the Earl of Surrey was stripped of his titles, attainted and imprisoned in the Tower of London by the victorious Henry VII of the house of Tudor.

Three years later, Thomas Howard (Mary's grandfather and her father's namesake) was released from the Tower and restored to the earldom of Surrey, although many of his lands were still under the King's custody. As the years passed by, Thomas Howard managed to carve out a successful career under Henry VII, eventually rising high in the royal favour; his son was even allowed to marry the Queen's sister, Anne of York. One of the earl's daughters, Elizabeth Howard, married Thomas Boleyn and bore him "every year a child" including the future queen, Anne Boleyn, who would play a significant role in Mary's life.[1]

The Earl of Surrey and his family thrived under the reign of Henry VIII, who succeeded his father in 1509. The earl's spectacular victory over the King of Scotland at Flodden in September 1513 earned him the King's respect and the restoration to the dukedom of Norfolk in February 1514. The earldom of Surrey passed on to his eldest son, Thomas, who had been widowed since 1512. Realizing fully well that his family's newly established power had to be consolidated through marriage with a woman of high birth, Thomas Howard decided to marry one of the Duke of Buckingham's daughters.

Edward Stafford, third Duke of Buckingham, was descended through his father from King Edward III. At that time, he was the only nobleman in England with a ducal status, and thus his daughters were valuable catches. Thomas Howard was especially attracted to the Duke of Buckingham's eldest daughter, Elizabeth, who was fifteen at the time. However, Elizabeth's hand in marriage had been promised to her father's ward, Ralph Neville, the Earl of

Westmorland's heir. "He and I loved together for two years", she would later recall, adding that had Thomas Howard not "made suit to my lord my father", she would have been married to Ralph Neville by the following Christmas.[2]

Buckingham was apparently prepared to offer one of his younger daughters to Thomas Howard, perhaps realizing that Elizabeth had feelings for Ralph. Thomas, however, was interested only in Elizabeth; "he would have none of my sisters, but only me", she later reminisced, adding that he "chose me for love". Thomas was twenty years her senior, and Elizabeth's own words only confirm that a medieval marriage was a business transaction and women were traded as commodities. "I was of his own choosing", she bemoaned, "and he not of mine".

On 21 May 1524, Mary's grandfather died at the ripe old age of eighty-one, and her father succeeded him as the third Duke of Norfolk, while the earldom of Surrey descended to Mary's elder brother, Henry. Children of aristocratic families were not raised by their parents, but by a staff of experienced women in the nursery. Aristocratic women were expected to bear as many children as they could in order to preserve their husbands' bloodline, but they were also expected to return to service at court. Mary, as other children of the Tudor aristocracy, was cared for by a wet nurse who fed her and then supervised by the lady governess. The Howards' main homes were Tendring Hall in Stoke by Nayland and Kenninghall Palace in Norfolk. The inventory of Kenninghall taken in December 1546 reveals that this redbrick palace situated on seven hundred acres boasted seventy rooms, including a great hall, presence chamber, nursery, chapel and wash-house. It was also staffed with a secretary, steward, treasurer, seneschal, almoner, personal physician and the children's tutor.[3]

As most noble families of the period, the Howards had more than one residence and often moved between their various estates depending on the season. A record of the trip from Tendring Hall to Hunsdon in the autumn of 1523 survives to this day and offers a tantalising glimpse of the aristocratic family on the move. The family and its household set off in the small hours of 29 October 1523, stopping at Easterford and Dunmow for breakfast and lunch, crossing the River Stort and reaching Hunsdon in the evening.[4] The four-year-old Mary Howard was probably too small to remember anything from this particular trip, but her childhood would have been dominated by similar tours.

But the life of the Howards was not always all about living in luxury in England. When Mary's father became

Lord Lieutenant of Ireland in 1520, he moved from England to Ireland, taking his family with him. There, the Howards were exposed to the hardships of war and plague, and when three of their household's members caught the sickness and died, Thomas Howard was eager to have his wife and children sent to safety:

"Most humbly, I beseech your grace to give me leave to send my wife and children into Wales or Lancashire to remain near the seaside until . . . it shall please God to cease this death here."[5]

However, this plea was rejected and Thomas Howard was recalled to England only when he had been badly afflicted with dysentery in 1521. Thomas's duties usually kept him busy with the King's wars in Ireland, France or at the Scottish borders, while his wife Elizabeth divided her time between supervising their household and serving as the Queen's lady-in-waiting.

Two household accounts dating from April 1523-January 1524 and September 1525 survive and reveal a glimpse into the daily life of the Howards. Breakfast in those days was served early, usually before the morning Mass at six or seven o'clock, and consisted of chicken and mutton. Supper in the Howard household consisted of an assortment of beef, lamb, goose, venison, rabbit, pig, veal, duck, pigeon, swan and various fishes.[6] The choice between meat and fish was determined by the liturgical calendar; eating meat was forbidden on Fridays and during Lent, and on such occasions, the Howards ate pike, tench, salmon and trout.[7] During their parents' absence, Mary's brother Henry would assume the role of formal host, sitting at the head of the table, resplendent in his best clothes.[8] How much the five-year-old Mary remembered from that period remains speculative, but she may have had some distant memories of costly dinners her parents threw while entertaining high-profile guests, including local gentry and bishops.

Most aristocratic families were accustomed to sending their children into households of their peers. The most revealing description of this custom, so typical to English noble families, was written by an Italian visitor to England in about the year 1500:

"The want of affection in the English is strongly manifested towards their children; for after having kept them at home till they arrive at the age of seven or nine years at the utmost, they put them out, both males and females, to hard service in the houses of other people, binding them generally for another seven or nine years. And these are called apprentices, and during that time they perform all the most menial offices; and few are born who are exempted from this fate, for everyone, however rich he may be, sends away his children into the houses of others, whilst he, in return, receives those of strangers into his own. And on inquiring their reason for this severity, they answered that they did it in order that their children might learn better manners."[9]

This Italian observer's judgement was clouded by what seemed to him as a cruel and unnatural way of raising children. Contrary to his opinion that they performed "the most menial offices", aristocratic children were not handled as servants per se, but treated with the respect of their birthright and counted as part of the family.[10] Surprisingly, neither Mary nor her brothers were sent away from home to join the households of other aristocratic families, as the available household accounts clearly show that they were raised in the Howard estates and cared for by a host of governesses and tutors.

There is only one child that appears to have made extended visits to the Howard estates on occasion: Katherine, Thomas Howard's daughter. The fact that she did not live with the other Howard children may point to the possibility that she was Thomas's illegitimate child, raised in the household of another aristocratic family.

Historian Beverley Murphy pointed out that Katherine "was at least twenty-two years old" in 1530, which places her birth at some point in 1508, during Thomas Howard's first marriage to Anne of York.[11] It is possible that Katherine was the product of an extramarital affair, but the fact that he secured an advantageous marriage for her and was devastated after her death may point to the possibility that she was Anne of York's daughter and thus the only surviving child from Thomas Howard's first marriage, although it is generally accepted by historians that the couple had no surviving children. The fact that Thomas's second wife, Elizabeth Stafford, displayed no interest in Katherine's marriage but was keen to have her say when it came to Mary's match, points to the strong possibility that Katherine was not Duchess Elizabeth's child.

In the first quarter of the sixteenth century, Thomas More formulated his ideas about the education of women and put them into practice in his own household; his daughter Margaret was one of the best educated women of the period. Mary Howard's older cousins, Anne and Mary Boleyn, were also very well educated. Mary's uncle, Thomas Boleyn, who was an ambassador and diplomat, afforded his two daughters an advanced education, securing them positions at the courts of Margaret of Austria and Francis I.

But Mary Howard was not sent to court until 1532 to attend Anne Boleyn, who, by then, was established as Henry VIII's queen-in-waiting. From this, we may infer that Mary was educated at home until she was thirteen years old.

A clear view of the extent of Mary Howard's education is impossible to attain, but there are some important clues that offer interesting glimpses into her schooling. She was taught to read and write, as several of her still-extant letters attest. Her handwriting, however, was far from perfect. The business letters she penned to influential members of the court are full of inkblots, deletions and spelling errors. Mary was aware that her style of writing was not as elegant or grammatical as one might expect from a woman of her rank, and in one of her surviving letters, she apologized to the recipient for "reading my evil [awful] hand". She also acknowledged her "travail in writing".[12] It was not uncommon, however, for educated aristocratic women to write and spell badly. It was a polite convention to plead inadequacy; Katherine Parr, for instance, wrote that one of her letters was "scribbled", although all of her surviving letters are written in fine Italianate hand.[13]

All aristocratic girls who aspired to become maids of honour were expected to master at least one foreign language, usually French. Mary Howard's grandfather commissioned a book about French grammar at the time when Mary and her brothers lived in Hunsdon Hall. The title of the book indicates that it was a manual "to write and pronounce French", and there is no indication that it was intended solely for the purpose of educating Mary's brothers.[14]

Historian Retha M. Warnicke has suggested that Mary Howard was educated as a classicist with her brother Henry, "a conclusion based primarily on evidence of her association with others who were learned".[15] Indeed, Mary and Henry were both associated with the circle that produced and frequently contributed to the *Devonshire Manuscript*, a courtly anthology. After her brother's execution for treason in 1547, Mary supervised the education of his children and was celebrated as "a woman of great wisdom" and patroness of the Reformers.[16]

Mary certainly received the solid training befitting a great lady in the making. Although mothers did not take active roles in the education of their children, they were expected to instruct their daughters in the traditional womanly pursuits such as sewing, embroidering and dancing. Riding, hunting and hawking were deemed very important as well. Two of Mary Howard's cousins who became Henry VIII's wives, Anne Boleyn and Katherine Howard, were highly skilled performers. Anne "knew perfectly how to sing and dance . . . to play the lute and other instruments", while Katherine was taught to play the lute and virginals when she was raised in the household of Agnes Howard, the Dowager Duchess of Norfolk.[17] Neither Anne Boleyn nor Katherine Howard were raised to become queens; they were, as was Mary Howard, groomed to become ornaments of the court and entertainers for the King's pleasure.

There is evidence that suggests that Duchess Elizabeth, Mary's mother, had a rather strict approach towards her children. When her brother asked if she could raise one of his daughters in her household, she replied:

"If you send me any of your daughters, I pray you to send me my niece Dorothy, for I am well acquainted with her conditions already, and so I am not with the others; and she is the youngest too; and if she be changed, therefore, she is better to break as concerning her youth."[18]

The comment about "breaking" Dorothy if her behaviour had changed for the worse is especially noteworthy because it reveals Elizabeth's attitude towards the harsh discipline imposed on children that characterised the Tudor society at that time. Wilfulness was considered a bad trait in a child, and parents were encouraged to supress it by any means.

NOTES

[1] Ives, *The Life and Death of Anne Boleyn*, p. 17.

[2] Everett-Wood, *Letters of Royal and Illustrious Ladies*, Volume 2, p. 361.

[3] Hutchinson, *House of Treason*, pp. 271-2.

[4] Childs, *Henry VIII's Last Victim*, pp. 20-1.

[5] Hutchinson, op.cit., p. 84.

[6] Howlett, *The Household Accounts*, pp. 53-60.

[7] Ibid., p. 53.

[8] Childs, op.cit., p. 30.

[9] Morgan, *Readings in English Social History*, p. 231.

[10] Evans, *Ladies-in-Waiting*, p. 19.

[11] Murphy, *Bastard Prince*, p. 124.

[12] Baron, *Mary Fitzroy's Hand in the Devonshire Manuscript*, p. 319.

[13] Harris, *English Aristocratic Women*, p. 35.

[14] Ibid., p. 261.

[15] Warnicke, *Women of the English Renaissance and Reformation*, p.38.

[16] Nichols, *Mary Richmond: Female Biographies of English History*, pp.480-87.

[17] Evans, op.cit., p. 25.

[18] Everett-Wood, *Letters of Royal and Illustrious Ladies*, Volume 3, p. 190.

CHAPTER 3:
THE HOWARDS AND THE ROYAL FAVOUR

When in the spring of 1527 Henry VIII decided to annul his marriage to Katherine of Aragon and marry one of her maids of honour, Mary Howard's mother sided with the Queen. The beginning of Henry VIII's so called Great Matter—that is, the annulment of his marriage to Katherine of Aragon—coincided with the Duke of Norfolk's taking a mistress.[1] As her private life demonstrated, the Duchess of Norfolk entertained the strongest views on marital fidelity and, just as she defied her husband's mistress, she defied Anne Boleyn and everything she stood for.

Anne Boleyn, the King's new love interest, was the daughter of the Duke of Norfolk's sister, Elizabeth Howard Boleyn, and thus his niece. Anne was not a paragon of beauty, although many acknowledged that her charm lay in her immaculate elegance and quick wit. Her swarthy complexion covered with small moles, as well as her black eyes and dark hair, were not the current fashion. Henry VIII, however, found her immensely attractive, as did poet

Thomas Wyatt and the Earl of Northumberland's heir, Henry Percy. Anne was clever, well educated, witty and ambitious. Seven years spent abroad gave her the continental gloss and aura of worldliness most of her female counterparts lacked.

When Anne caught the King's eye sometime in 1526, he intended to make her his mistress, but Anne steadfastly refused. Her enemies speculated that "she learned from the example of her sister" how the King's affection towards his mistresses changed.[2] Indeed, Anne's elder sister, Mary Boleyn, was Henry VIII's mistress and, according to contemporary hearsay, bore him at least one child.

When the word spread that the King wanted to marry the sister of his former mistress, people were outraged. The King always emphasized that he held his marriage to Katherine of Aragon as unlawful because she was his brother's widow, although the Queen always maintained that her short-lived marriage to Prince Arthur had never been consummated. The rules of sixteenth-century canon law may be difficult to understand today, but they were part of everyday life at the time. People in Henry VIII's England believed that, just as it was wrong to marry one's brother's wife, it was equally wrong to marry one's former mistress's sister.

In both cases, the question of so-called "carnal knowledge" presented an obstacle. Anne Boleyn was thus related to Henry VIII by affinity, and a papal dispensation was required for them to marry. Like Henry VIII's contemporaries, modern historians agree that it was an extraordinarily bold step. According to historian Giles Tremlett, "The double standard was remarkable". Tremlett pointed out that whereas Henry disputed the validity of the papal dispensation allowing him to marry his brother's widow, he saw nothing wrong in seeking it to marry his former mistress's sister.[3] Despite murmurings at court, the King insisted that his desire to marry Anne Boleyn was "founded upon justice" and not rooted in some "undue love".

The English ambassadors who visited the pope in 1528 praised Anne's "constant virginity" and many other laudable qualities, such as her "apparent aptness to procreation of children".[4] Women of the court disapproved of the King's relationship with Anne Boleyn, who was perceived as a social climber and—although she refused to warm the royal bed—as Henry VIII's "whore". One of the resident ambassadors opined that "if the matter [of the King's annulment] were decided by women, the King would lose the battle".[5] As it soon became evident, even Anne's family was not unanimously in favour of displacing the Queen, and Mary Howard's mother emerged as one of the most high-profile supporters of Katherine of Aragon.

The Duchess of Norfolk strongly disliked her husband's niece and made demonstrations of her undying support for Queen Katherine. There is plenty of evidence that she considered herself to be superior to Anne Boleyn in terms of noble origin. As a daughter of the ducal magnate, albeit executed for treason in 1521, Duchess Elizabeth was a descendant of King Edward III's youngest son, Thomas Woodstock, and of John of Gaunt. Her father was beheaded because he was considered a threat to Henry VIII's succession, so the duchess was well aware of her high birth. At some point, she even argued with Queen Katherine because she allowed the Dowager Duchess of Norfolk to take precedence over her.[6] Therefore, it must have been a heavy blow to the Duchess of Norfolk when on 8 December 1529, Anne Boleyn's father, whom she considered an upstart, was ennobled, receiving the double title of Earl of Wiltshire and Ormond, the former being previously held by the duchess's uncle, Henry Stafford.

The next day, a grand feast was thrown to celebrate the triumph of Anne's father and, as the imperial ambassador reported, Anne Boleyn, who held no noble title on her own at the time, sat by the King's side, occupying the Queen's place, and took precedence over all highborn ladies, such as the Duchess of Norfolk herself, the Dowager Duchess of Norfolk and even Henry VIII's sister, Mary Tudor Brandon.

Over a year later, Duchess Elizabeth's displeasure over Anne Boleyn's exaltation was widely known and commented upon within court circles. The imperial ambassador reported that someone informed him that Duchess Elizabeth ridiculed the elaborated family tree which claimed the Boleyns were an old and noble family. The ambassador's informant claimed that Duchess Elizabeth told Anne that such a fabricated family tree was laughable.[7] It remains unknown what exactly this family tree contained.

Anne Boleyn's influence grew steadily, and in October 1529, rumour had it that she had convinced Henry VIII to arrange a marriage between his daughter, Princess Mary, and the Duke of Norfolk's son—Mary Howard's brother—Henry, Earl of Surrey.[8] Tying Henry VIII's daughter to her relative would ensure control over the princess, who was the King's only legitimate child and, until the birth of a legitimate brother, heiress to the throne. It would have also ensured that no foreign groom would claim the princess in the future.

According to the imperial ambassador, the marriage between the Earl of Surrey and Princess Mary could have been to Queen Katherine's advantage since the Duke of Norfolk would then switch his allegiance and support Princess Mary's mother instead of Anne Boleyn.[9] In fact, however, the Duke of Norfolk had more reasons to support Anne Boleyn, his niece, since they both had common interests, such as neutralizing Cardinal Wolsey, and there was no sign of the King tiring of Anne just yet.

The Duke of Norfolk, however, might have deliberately sought to hold a leg in both camps, giving outward appearances of supporting Anne Boleyn while employing his wife to open a secret communication with the discarded Queen. In November 1530, the Duchess of Norfolk sent Queen Katherine a gift of poultry with an orange containing a hidden message from the English ambassador in Rome. Although Katherine of Aragon believed that the duchess sent this gift "out of love and affection she bears her", the imperial ambassador believed "that all has been done with the duke's knowledge; at all events this seems to open a way for the Queen to communicate more freely with her friends and disclose her plans to the duchess".[10] Later events, however, seem to prove that the imperial ambassador was wrong in his assertions because the Duchess of Norfolk never ceased to support Queen Katherine, even when it was more advantageous for her family's interests to switch her allegiance to Anne Boleyn.

In stark contrast to the Duchess of Norfolk, Mary Howard's step-grandmother, Agnes Howard, Dowager Duchess of Norfolk, decided to support Anne Boleyn. Agnes Howard was one of the richest and most influential noblewomen in England. She ran a household for young noblewomen within her estates at Lambeth and Horsham—Henry VIII's fifth wife, Katherine Howard, was under her care—and she was present at Thomas Boleyn's ennoblement feast in December 1529.

Agnes was one of the noblewomen who had witnessed the naissance of the Tudor dynasty, so in some sense, she was a relic of the past. Agnes remembered Katherine of Aragon's marriage to Prince Arthur in 1501, and she gave her deposition when the issue of the Queen's first marriage's consummation was weighed in court. Agnes Howard testified that Katherine of Aragon and Prince Arthur "were brought to bed" the next night after their marriage, and she saw them "lying in one bed the same night, in a chamber within the said palace being prepared for them". Agnes said nothing about the consummation itself, as she had no knowledge of that, but she said that she "left them so lying together there the said night".[11] The Dowager Duchess's deposition was apparently enough to earn her the King's gratitude, and she would become one of the most important supporters of Anne Boleyn and the honoured guest at court banquets held in Anne's honour.

There is no source that would throw some light upon Agnes's relationship with her step-granddaughter Mary, but they certainly knew each other socially and met on several occasions, including Anne Boleyn's coronation in 1533.

NOTES

[1] This subject is discussed in Chapter 11.
[2] Pole, *Defense of the Unity of the Church*, p. 185.
[3] Tremlett, *Catherine of Aragon*, p. 282.
[4] *Letters and Papers*, Volume 4, n. 3913.
[5] Ibid., n. 5702.
[6] *Calendar of State Papers, Spain*, Volume 4 Part 1, n. 232.
[7] Friedmann, *Anne Boleyn: A Chapter of English History 1527–1536*, Volume 1, pp. 37, 128.
[8] *Calendar of State Papers, Spain*, Volume 4 Part 1, n. 182.
[9] Ibid., n. 232.
[10] Ibid., n. 509.
[11] *Letters and Papers*, Volume 4, n. 5778.

CHAPTER 4:
INTO THE MARRIAGE MARKET

Thomas Howard was well aware that all of his children were valuable commodities in the marriage market. In April 1523, when Mary Howard was only four years old, her father was already thinking about her future and sought a wardship of Lord Monteagle, hoping to obtain the young man for one of his two daughters.[1] Neither of his daughters, however, was married until the late 1520s. Katherine Howard, Norfolk's elder daughter (not to be confused with his niece, who later became Queen), contracted a marriage to Edward Stanley, Earl of Derby, in 1529. Derby was a minor under the King's authority, and the Duke, desperate to obtain him for Katherine, was obliged to seek pardon on 21 February 1530 "for the abduction of Edward Earl of Derby and [his] marriage to Katherine, daughter of the said Thomas, without royal licence".[2]

Unfortunately, Katherine died of plague on 15 March 1530. The imperial ambassador reported that Katherine's death "will be one of the greatest blows the duke has ever received", but he did not pinpoint whether that was because Norfolk was so fond of his daughter or whether he was merely afraid to lose an ally. [3] Norfolk did not wish to "let this alliance slip", so he arranged a papal dispensation for one of his sisters to marry Derby.[4] The imperial ambassador picked up a rumour that claimed if Norfolk had no sister to offer to Derby, he "would have proposed to him his other daughter, who has been promised to the Duke of Richmond".[5] Mary Howard's reaction to her elder sister's death remains unknown, as we have virtually no information about the relationship between the two.

Mary's mother wished to see her daughter married to the Earl of Derby and spoke up against her match with Henry Fitzroy, Duke of Richmond. Anne Boleyn was eager to see Mary married to Fitzroy and overruled the Duchess of Norfolk, using "such high words" towards her that "the latter narrowly escaped being dismissed from court".[6] The Duchess would later reminisce that "Queen Anne got the marriage [with Fitzroy] clear for my lord my husband" when she favoured him.[7]

Mary was eleven at the time her relatives argued over her future; how much she understood and what she felt about the marriage to Henry VIII's illegitimate son remains unknown. What we do know is that by March 1531, the marriage negotiations had been fully concluded and must have been publicly announced since the imperial ambassador was referring to Fitzroy as the Duke of Norfolk's son-in-law.[8]

Despite the fact that Mary Howard was now Henry VIII's future daughter-in-law, her mother still fomented trouble. In April 1531, the feisty Duchess of Norfolk confided to Queen Katherine that her husband opined that Anne Boleyn "would be the ruin of her family".[9] At that time, Anne had been waiting for Henry VIII's divorce for four years, and the court was abuzz with rumours that she bemoaned her lost time and youth. Indeed, she was already thirty years old and entertained fears that the King would eventually give up on divorce and cast her aside.[10] The regular altercations and tearful making up between the King and his mistress were a constant part of their volatile relationship. Even the imperial ambassador Chapuys, always eagerly awaiting signs of the relationship's decline, dismissed such rows as "lovers' quarrels".[11] But Anne was getting irritated, and in May 1531, she secured the Duchess of Norfolk's exile from court. Chapuys noted that the duchess was sent home because she "spoke too freely and declared herself more than they [Henry and Anne] liked for the Queen."[12]

The Duchess of Norfolk's aversion towards Anne Boleyn reflected badly on the latter's reputation. Who would support Anne if not the members of her own family? Everyone involved in the conflict between the two, including the Duke of Norfolk, was aware of this quarrel's serious political ramifications and the message it carried to courtiers and resident ambassadors. Perhaps the Duke of Norfolk, perceiving that lending further support to Queen Katherine was pointless, decided to try to convince his wife to switch her allegiance to Anne Boleyn. Norfolk's letter dated 21 August 1532 indicates that there were plans for his wife to take part in Anne's ennoblement ceremony. The original intention was to provide crimson velvet for three countesses' gowns, but this plan changed quickly. "The King's pleasure now is", wrote Norfolk, "that no robes of estate shall be now made but only for my wife".[13]

If Henry VIII and the Duke of Norfolk believed they could change the duchess's mind about Anne Boleyn, they were very much mistaken, for she ostentatiously did not appear at the ceremony. The honour of carrying Anne Boleyn's crimson velvet mantle and gold coronet on 1 September 1532 was given to thirteen-year-old Mary Howard instead. It was the first recorded ceremony in which Mary took part, and it marked the beginning of her career as Anne Boleyn's maid of honour.

NOTES

[1] In his letter to Thomas Wolsey, Norfolk asked him to beseech the King so that "I might have the young man to marry unto one of my daughters". (Bapst, *Deux Gentilhommes-Poètes de la Cour de Henry VIII*, p. 172.)

[2] Murphy, *Bastard Prince*, p. 124.

[3] *Calendar of State Papers, Spain,* Volume 4 Part 1, n. 270.

[4] Ibid., n. 460.

[5] Ibid.

[6] Ibid.

[7] Everett-Wood, *Letters of Royal and Illustrous Ladies*, Volume 2, p. 363.

[8] *Calendar of State Papers, Spain,* Volume 4 Part 2, n. 664.

[9] *Letters and Papers*, Volume 5, n. 216.

[10] *Calendar of State Papers, Spain,* Volume 4 Part 1, n. 224.

[11] Ibid., Volume 5 Part 1, n. 118.

[12] *Letters and Papers*, Volume 5, n. 238.

[13] Ibid., n. 1239.

Chapter 5:
Carving out a career

It must have been an unforgettable experience for Mary Howard to walk behind Anne Boleyn, carrying the mantle of crimson velvet furred with ermines and a coronet that Anne would put on her head after receiving the title of Marchioness of Pembroke. Glittering with the royal jewels and adorned with a matching surcoat of crimson velvet furred with ermine, Anne approached the King, kneeled, and received a patent of creation.[1] She was the first woman who received a noble title in her own right; usually, women gained courtesy titles by marriage.

Ennobling Anne Boleyn was only the first step to her international recognition. In October 1532, Henry VIII took her to Calais in order to present her to King Francis I as the future Queen of England. Rumour had it that Anne would be accompanied by thirty noblewomen, including the Duchess of Norfolk and the King's sister, Mary Tudor Brandon. In the end, however, only twelve ladies accompanied her, and neither the Duchess of Norfolk nor the King's sister lent their support to Henry VIII's future wife. The French noblewomen would not greet Anne Boleyn either; Francis

I's second wife was Eleanor of Austria, Katherine of Aragon's niece, so her presence was understandably out of the question. Even the French King's sister, Marguerite of Navarre, whom Anne Boleyn respected and fondly remembered from her time at the French court, pleaded ill health and unexpectedly withdrew from the meeting.[2]

But Anne had her supporters and spared no expense to enhance their appearance by her side. On 27 October 1532, she selected six of her female attendants and all, clad in cloth of gold, crimson satin and cloth of silver, with masks covering their faces, entered the hall decorated with expensive tapestries where Francis I and Henry VIII held a lavish banquet. The ladies danced and turned towards the spectators, then selected dancing partners.

Wynkyn de Worde's semi-official propagandistic pamphlet entitled *The Manner of the Triumph at Calais and Boulogne* listed the ladies who danced with Anne that evening. Anne, at the head, was followed by "my Lady Mary", who was important enough to take precedence over the remaining ladies, including a countess.[3] Some historians argue that "my Lady Mary" was none other than Anne's sister, Mary Boleyn Carey, but it seems highly unlikely that she would have taken precedence over ladies of higher rank, herself being only a widow of a mere knight. In her book, *Mary Boleyn: The Great and Infamous Whore*, Alison Weir opined that Mary Boleyn Carey was given precedence to "underline the fact that her sister was soon to be the Queen of England" and added that Mary Howard was also present during the meeting.[4]

In fact, however, Wynkyn de Worde's pamphlet, quoted by Weir as a source, points out that there was only one "Lady Mary" dancing along Anne Boleyn that evening. The mysterious "Lady Mary" could not have been Mary Tudor Brandon since she was referred to as "the French Queen" by her contemporaries, and in any case, she strongly disapproved of her brother's relationship with Anne Boleyn.[5]

Eric Ives opined that "my Lady Mary" would "normally indicate Princess Mary", and therefore the news sent to England from Calais was deliberately distorted to create a rumour that Henry VIII's daughter was not opposed to her father's marriage to Anne Boleyn.[6] In 1532, however, Mary was still officially recognized and referred to as princess; she came to be known as "Lady Mary", degraded from the position of a princess only after Anne Boleyn gave birth to her daughter in September the following year. Therefore, the only noblewoman who could follow Anne Boleyn and take precedence over other ladies was Mary Howard.

Mary's presence at Calais seemed more than appropriate since she was affianced to Henry VIII's illegitimate son, Henry Fitzroy, who also accompanied the royal entourage, and her father and brothers were present as well. Henry Fitzroy was to remain in the entourage of Francis I's son, the Dauphin of France, for about a year to guarantee that his royal father would keep the terms of the treaty just signed. He was to be accompanied by his friend and Mary's brother, Henry Howard; they would not return home until September 1533.

The English entourage left Calais on 12 November 1532. Earlier departure was impossible due to the violent autumn storms at sea. It was a very slow crossing of twenty-nine hours, and when the King and his entourage returned, the *Te Deum* was sung at Saint Paul's Cathedral in thanksgiving. Henry VIII and Anne Boleyn did not return straight to court, however, and reached Eltham Palace by 24 November.

Anne Boleyn's place as Henry VIII's consort was now taken for granted. She was reportedly "living like a Queen" in Calais and at last allowed Henry VIII to become her lover in the fullest sense. At some point during their Calais trip, Anne surrendered her chastity and, as it soon would turn out, became pregnant. The marriage was contracted secretly in front of very few witnesses, although there is no conclusive evidence as to when it actually occurred. Chronicler Edward Hall recorded that Henry VIII married Anne Boleyn shortly after returning from Calais, "on Saint Erkenwald's Day [14 November 1532]" while Thomas Cranmer wrote that they married "about St. Paul's day last", that is, about 25 January 1533.[7]

On 12 April 1533, Henry VIII ended the speculation and flaunted Anne Boleyn as Queen before the entire court. Clad in cloth of gold and "loaded with the richest jewels", Anne was accompanied by sixty maids of honour and ceremonially led to Mass; the long train of her gown was carried by Mary Howard.[8]

In late May 1533, the King's first marriage was pronounced null and void, and his marriage to Anne Boleyn was recognized as valid. Anne's pregnancy was already starting to show, and the imperial ambassador observed that she added a panel to the front of her gown to accommodate her growing girth. Several days later, Anne—six months pregnant and resplendent in the finest cloths and jewels—was crowned as the new Queen of England.

Anne's chariot, bedecked with cloth of silver, was followed by four chariots containing ladies of her household and other gentlewomen on horseback dressed in crimson velvet. Although the complete list of Anne Boleyn's attendants is not extant, we may assume that Mary Howard was among them.

After her coronation, Anne took measures to ensure the highest standards within her household. William Latymer, the Queen's chaplain, later recalled how she assembled her ladies-in-waiting and maids of honour in her Privy Chamber and delivered a powerful speech imploring her female servants to "use themselves [behave] according to their calling". Anne would "commonly and generally many times move [encourage] them to modesty and chastity". The Queen was especially concerned with her maids of honours' well-being because they were young, inexperienced and the most vulnerable at court. To ensure their good behaviour, Anne gathered her maids in her Privy Chamber "and before the Mother of Maids, would give them a long charge of their behaviours".[9]

Known for her leanings towards the New Religion, Anne encouraged her ladies to read the Bible in vernacular and allowed them access to her own copy of William Tyndale's English translation of the New Testament, which

45

she held opened at her desk within her Privy Chamber. Later, people would recall that there was "never a better order among ladies and gentlewomen than during Queen Anne's time".

On 26 August 1533, the Queen entered her confinement for "lying-in". There is no information about the ladies who served Anne Boleyn in her confinement, but we may assume that Mary Howard, Margaret Douglas and Mary Shelton, who were unmarried, were not allowed to enter this sanctum. They were, however, present at the magnificent christening ceremony of the newly born Princess Elizabeth on 10 September 1533. Carried under a canopy of estate by the Dowager Duchess of Norfolk, Elizabeth was wrapped in a mantle of purple velvet with a long train. Mary Howard carried a "chrisom of pearl and stone" to put on the child at baptism.[10]

After the birth and christening, life at court went on as normal, but for Mary Howard, Margaret Douglas and Mary Shelton, the autumn of 1533 was especially significant. Mary Howard's young fiancé, Henry Fitzroy, returned home from France in September, and their wedding was planned to take place in November. As for Margaret Douglas, the birth of Elizabeth changed her position in the household of Princess Mary.

The newly born Princess Elizabeth was perceived—if not by the majority at court, then at least by her parents and their adherents—as the rightful heiress to the throne. Within a week of her birth, the King was pressing his elder daughter, Princess Mary, to stop using the title of princess. She was to be henceforth known as "the Lady Mary, the King's daughter".[11] Mary refused to accept her new position, and she blamed Anne Boleyn rather than Henry VIII for the change in her status. While Mary emphasized that she would accept Elizabeth as her illegitimate sister, just as she had accepted Henry Fitzroy as her illegitimate brother, she would never acknowledge the infant as a princess, for this title belonged to her and to her only.

Margaret Douglas, who appeared among Mary's "ladies and gentlewomen" on an October 1533 checkroll, witnessed her cousin's degradation and saw its impact on Mary as a firsthand witness.[12] Mary's chamberlain, John Hussey, observed that her servants were prepared to accept the new status of their royal mistress because "they will always be ready to obey the King, saving their conscience".[13] Mary's governess, Margaret Pole, Countess of Salisbury, offered to serve Mary at her own expense but was rejected by the King, who already had a replacement in mind.

In December 1533, Princess Elizabeth was provided with her own royal household and transferred with "pompous solemnity" to her new home in the countryside.[14] Anne Boleyn wanted to surround her daughter with members of her own family, and she appointed her father's sister, Anne Shelton, as Elizabeth's governess. Anne Shelton was the mother of Mary Shelton, who served as one of the Queen's maids of honour. As for Henry VIII's elder daughter, she was to live in Elizabeth's establishment under the stewardship of Anne Boleyn's relatives. Although she was still recognized as the King's child, Lady Mary's estate was respectable but clearly distinguished from that of Elizabeth's. The imperial ambassador reported that Mary was to be treated as Elizabeth's servant.

It remains unknown when exactly Margaret Douglas left the household of Mary Tudor, or if she had ever became a part of the combined household of Mary and Elizabeth, but in March 1534, her presence was already noticed at court. The French ambassador Castillion reported that Lady Mary's defiance did not matter much for Henry VIII because "there were many other girls in his kingdom", including his niece Margaret. Although the King was trying to play Mary's defiance down, in reality he was angry about her blatant disrespect of his parental and kingly authority. Henry brought up Margaret's name in a conversation with Castillion because he wanted to emphasize that Mary, as his illegitimate daughter, was now technically below her cousin Margaret in the newly established order. According to Castillion, Margaret Douglas was much made of at court; the King "keeps [her] with the Queen his wife, and treats [her] like a queen's daughter".

The French ambassador also added that if Henry VIII were to offer Margaret's hand in marriage to anyone, "he would make her marriage worth as much as his daughter Mary's". The ambassador was clearly impressed with Margaret, reporting that "the lady is beautiful and highly esteemed here".[15] The King was subtly insinuating that Margaret Douglas had somehow replaced Lady Mary in his policies, although it was not entirely true. While Margaret's support of Henry VIII's marriage to Anne Boleyn was welcome and meaningful, Mary's intransigence was still perceived as an insult to Henry and Anne.

It is possible that Margaret Douglas transferred to Anne Boleyn's household shortly before the arrival of Sir Adam Otterburn, the Scottish ambassador to England, in March 1534. In fact, Margaret's exaltation at court may have been very closely connected to this particular visit. Otterburn paid a visit to Anne Boleyn and, although we do not know anything about the conversations that passed between them, the sight of the Dowager Queen of Scotland's daughter among Anne's ladies must have made him feel welcome.

NOTES

[1] *Calendar of State Papers, Venice,* Volume 4, n. 802.

[2] Ives, *The Life and Death of Anne Boleyn,* p. 157.

[3] The whole list included Anne Boleyn, Marquess of Pembroke; Dorothy Howard, Countess of Derby and Elizabeth Howard, Lady Fitzwalter (Anne's aunts); Jane Parker, Lady Rochford (Anne's sister-in-law); Honor Grenville, Lady Lisle (wife of the governor of Calais); and Elizabeth Harleston, Lady Wallop (wife of the English ambassador to France), [Letters and Papers, Volume 5, n. 1484]

[4] Weir, *Mary Boleyn,* p. 252.

[5] Ives, op.cit., p. 390.
Calendar of State Papers, Venice, Volume 4, n. 761.

[6] Ives, op.cit., p. 161.

[7] *Letters and Papers,* Volume 6, n. 661.

[8] *Calendar of State Papers, Venice,* Volume 4, n. 870.

[9] Latymer, *Cronickille of Anne Bulleyne,* Volume 39 of Camden Fourth Series, p. 63.

[10] *Letters and Papers,* Volume 6, n. 1111.

[11] Ibid., n. 1207.

[12] Ibid., n. 1199.

[13] Ibid., n. 1139.

[14] *Calendar of State Papers, Spain,* Volume 4 Part 2, n. 1161.

[15] *Letters and Papers,* Volume 7, n. 13.

Chapter 6: Marriage to the King's Son

Henry Fitzroy was born in June 1519 and was the only illegitimate son that Henry VIII ever acknowledged. His mother was Elizabeth "Bessie" Blount, the King's mistress, who was later married off to Gilbert Tailboys. The King doted on his only son and created him Duke of Richmond and Somerset in June 1525, providing him with a magnificent household. On 3 September 1533, the imperial ambassador reported that Fitzroy returned home from the French court "to marry the daughter of Norfolk", Mary Howard.[1]

The wedding took place on 25 November, and there seemed to be no great celebrations at court; we only know that the wedding went as planned from the footnote in Eustace Chapuys's dispatch.[2] What the two fourteen-year-olds thought about each other remains unknown. It is possible that they started their relationship on a friendly note, considering that Mary Howard's brother Henry, Earl of Surrey, was Fitzroy's best friend, and her father had become the boy's advisor and guardian after Cardinal Wolsey's death in 1530. There is some evidence that when Fitzroy and Surrey were growing up together, they passed their time with "the ladies bright of hue" and pursued them in a manner of courtly love.[3] These relationships were probably platonic, however.

Portraits of Henry Fitzroy and Mary Howard survive and show that they were an attractive pair. In an unfinished sketch by Hans Holbein, the auburn-haired Mary wears a bonnet with a feather and has downturned eyes. The drawing is inscribed by the artist: "red velvet" and "black velvet", indicating materials of her gown. Henry Fitzroy was painted by Lucas Horenbout; in his miniature, he appears to be dressed informally in his linen shirt, with the high collar left undone, and a close-fitting embroidered cap. Fitzroy's resemblance to Henry VIII is striking; he has grey eyes, pale skin and reddish eyebrows. Contemporaries often remarked upon Fitzroy's resemblance to Henry VIII; he was described as "a youth of great promise, so much does he resemble his father".[4] There's also evidence that apart from good looks and many accomplishments, Fitzroy inherited his father's short temper: one of the boy's servants later confessed that he lived in "fear of blows that happened in his rage".[5] Fitzroy's inclination towards physical violence may have been a matter of upbringing rather than an inbred trait, however.

Mary Howard and her young husband were not allowed to consummate their relationship and lived in separate households, seeing each other at court from time to time. Marriages in sixteenth-century England required consummation in order to be legal, and sometimes, when the spouses were young, they were permitted to consummate the marriage on their wedding night and then they abstained from sexual intercourse for several years. This was the case in 1501, when Henry VII made a decision that his fifteen-year-old son Arthur "will know his wife sexually on the day of the wedding and then separate himself from her for two or three years because it is said that the prince is frail, and the King . . . wanted to have them [Arthur and Katherine of Aragon] with him for the first three years [of their marriage] so that the prince should mature in strength".[6] These requirements were grounded in concern for Arthur because the surfeit of sexual activity at an early age was believed to lead to an early death. Katherine of Aragon's brother died in 1497, aged nineteen, of what his contemporaries believed was overenthusiastic lovemaking. Mary Howard and Henry Fitzroy were fourteen at the time of their marriage, and it is reasonable to assume that Henry VIII was afraid to lose his only son and decided to prohibit sexual intercourse.

Mary continued in the Queen's service while Fitzroy attended court during feasts and occasions of state. During the festive season of 1533-34, Fitzroy exchanged gifts with Henry VIII and Anne Boleyn on New Year's Day. His presence at court was not only a testament to the King's virility but also a constant reminder to Queen Anne of what was expected of her. Early in 1534, the Queen had cause for celebration because she was with child again, and the new Act of Succession strengthened her position as Henry VIII's wife and mother of heirs to the throne.

In the summer of 1534, the court went on a royal progress; Mary Howard went with the Queen's household while her husband went on to travel through his own lands, where he was received by local dignitaries. If Mary Howard and Henry Fitzroy exchanged letters when they were apart, they did not survive, but there is a hint that Mary's father, the Duke of Norfolk, tried to keep the couple close together. When the court returned from the summer progress in September 1534, the imperial ambassador reported that Norfolk desired "to keep the Duke of Richmond near him and near his daughter, his wife".[7] Perhaps Norfolk was hoping that now, when Anne Boleyn's pregnancy ended in stillbirth, any child born to Mary and Fitzroy would be a good insurance policy for the future.

Over a year later, rumours reached Paris that Anne Boleyn and her adherents suspected that Norfolk wanted to marry his son, Surrey, to Lady Mary Tudor.[8] Several years earlier, it had been Anne's idea to marry her cousin to the King's elder daughter, but now Anne saw that Norfolk was two-faced and was pursuing his own agenda behind her back. In fact, however, Norfolk didn't have to make such grand plans; he already had the King's illegitimate son married to his daughter. Now all he had to do was wait until this union bore fruit.

NOTES

[1] *Letters and Papers*, Volume 6, n. 1069.
[2] Ibid., n. 1460.
[3] Norton, *Bessie Blount*, p. 256.
[4] *Calendar of State Papers, Venice*, Volume 4, n. 694.
[5] Strickland, *Lives of the Queens of England*, Volume 4, p. 133.
[6] Williams, *Katherine of Aragon*, p. 101.
[7] *Calendar of State Papers, Spain,* Volume 5 Part 1, n. 87.
[8] *Letters and Papers*, Volume 8, n. 985.

CHAPTER 7:
THE KING'S MISTRESS

Ever since Anne Boleyn's second pregnancy ended in mysterious circumstances—the natural conclusion is that she had given birth to a stillborn child or that the baby died soon after what seems to have been a premature labour—the King looked at her through a different lens. She was no longer an attractive and elusive mistress whose volatile temper and quick wit added to her charm. In Henry's view, Anne had become a nagging wife, always jealous of his new amours and unable to provide him with a son. Disillusioned with Anne, Henry sought consolation with other women.

In the autumn of 1534, he pursued an unnamed young woman who was dubbed by historians as "the Imperial Lady" due to her political sympathies. She served as Anne Boleyn's lady-in-waiting, but refused to pay honours to the Queen and made much of her support of Henry VIII's elder daughter, the bastardized Lady Mary. Anne was aware that this new rival of hers was championed by Anne's political enemies and tried to dismiss her. The Queen's plan failed, however, and she incurred the King's wrath. In the end, the romance with the "Imperial Lady" dissolved after six months when Henry VIII tired of her.

He was not lonely for long because on 25 February 1535, the imperial ambassador Chapuys reported that "the young lady who was lately in the King's favour is so no longer. There has succeeded to her place a cousin of the Concubine [Anne Boleyn], daughter of the present governess of the Princess [Mary Tudor]".[1] The governess in question who crops up often in Chapuys's dispatches was Anne Shelton, née Boleyn, sister of Queen Anne Boleyn's father, Thomas.

The Queen favoured and trusted the Sheltons, bestowing lucrative posts on them. John Shelton, who married Anne Boleyn's aunt around 1512, became the steward of the royal establishment where Princess Elizabeth and Lady Mary Tudor had lived since early 1534. It was the combined household of two daughters of Henry VIII, albeit Mary's state had been reduced from princess to a mere lady, acknowledged as the King's illegitimate child and not as his rightful heiress.

John and Anne Shelton had a large family of several children, including two daughters, Mary and Margaret, who attracted notable scholarly attention.[2] Mary Shelton contributed to the *Devonshire Manuscript*, a collection of 185 poems containing original and transcribed verses. Some entries, however, are not mere poems but "rather such ephemeral jottings as single names, ciphers, anagrams, pen-trials, and brief expressions of good will".[3] Circulating among the young, cultured and poetry-loving male and female courtiers, the *Devonshire Manuscript* served not only as a notebook filled with poems but also as a communication tool in which readers could participate directly and insert their own notes, giving each other advice, exchanging opinions and, most importantly, flirting in the convention of courtly love. Mary Shelton, together with Margaret Douglas and Mary Howard, was among the most prominent contributors to the *Devonshire Manuscript*; her hand can be clearly distinguished as she left her signature and provided a certified sample of her handwriting.

Establishing Mary Shelton's historical identity has become something of a difficulty among historians. Paul G. Remley, author of the most comprehensive scholarly article about Mary Shelton and her poetical achievements, rightfully pointed out that Mary's "historical identity has been misconstrued frequently by literary scholars".[4] In modern historical studies, Mary Shelton is often confused with her sister Margaret. Supposedly, the confusion arose from the label "Marg Shelton", making "Mary" look like "Marg" for Margaret. Instances where a *Y* resembled a *G* were common in sixteenth-century handwriting. While some historians still incorrectly ascertain that Margaret Shelton was the King's mistress in 1535, recent research has suggested that it was Mary Shelton who became Henry VIII's love interest at the time, as she often crops up in the courtly reports, while references to Margaret are very rare.

Mary Shelton's exact date of birth remains unknown. Her parents married circa 1512, and this is the earliest possible date of her birth. The earliest reference to Mary at court occurred in January 1534 when "Mistress Shelton" was listed as a recipient of a royal gift.[5] She was certainly Anne Boleyn's maid of honour at the time, and it is possible that she entered her household in the spring of 1533, when Anne's household was first formed. If Mary was sixteen years old at the time—a minimum age required for a post of maid of honour—then we can place her birth in or around the year 1518. This tactic of defining Mary Shelton's age may be misleading, however. As the Queen's cousin, she may have been favoured more than other girls and could have been younger than sixteen, just as Mary Howard was when she became Anne Boleyn's maid at the age of thirteen.

In any case, Mary Shelton was certainly much younger than Anne Boleyn, perhaps in her late teens or early twenties at the time when Henry VIII cast an appreciative eye on her.

Although it has been suggested by some historians that Mary Shelton was introduced to Henry VIII by the Boleyns, or even that the Queen herself pushed her young cousin into the King's arms in order to ensure that someone she could trust occupied her husband's bed, there is no evidence to that effect. Mary Shelton's relationship with Anne Boleyn is hard to evaluate, as there are almost no sources to base conclusions upon. Considering that Anne was extremely jealous of Henry VIII's mistresses and that she conspired to get rid of Mary Shelton's predecessor, we may only suspect that she was not too happy about Mary becoming her husband's lover. On the other hand, Anne might have been aware that just as the "Imperial Lady" had her own political agenda and supporters who backed her, Mary Shelton was a relative and someone whose well-being at court rested on the Boleyn Queen's good fortunes. Mary was thus unlikely to conspire against Anne Boleyn, as other women at court were.

The only anecdote that gives colour and dimension to Mary Shelton's relationship with Anne Boleyn is preserved in the account of the Queen's chaplain. In his

Cronickille of Anne Bulleyne, William Latymer recorded how on one occasion Anne Boleyn "wonderfully rebuked" Mary Shelton for doodling "idle poesies" in her prayer book. Such "wanton toys", as the Queen termed Mary's jottings, should not be scribbled in a prayer book, "mirror or glass wherein she might learn to address her wandering thoughts".[6]

At first glance, the Queen's outburst looks like it was motivated by Mary Shelton's spiritual well-being, but the analysis of other factors throws an entirely different light on this incident. During their courtship, Anne Boleyn and Henry VIII exchanged love notes in a prayer book. In *Mistresses of Henry VIII*, author Kelly Hart suggested that Anne Boleyn's real concern might have been that "Mary's poetry was for the King".[7] This scenario is certainly possible.

Another explanation may be that Mary attracted the attention of Anne's erstwhile suitor, the poet Thomas Wyatt. One of Wyatt's poems in the *Devonshire Manuscript* is addressed to Mary Shelton and implores her to respond to his advances. Each line of the poem is spelled out "Sheltun" in a similar way that an earlier poem written for Anne Boleyn was spelled "Anna". There was certainly a flirtation between Thomas Wyatt and Mary Shelton, as Mary wrote "forget this" beside the poem. The nature of

Mary's replies may suggest that Wyatt's feelings were unrequited.[8]

The nature of the relationship between Mary Shelton and Henry VIII is equally difficult to define. Mary was a young and good-looking girl, resembling the famous beauty Christina, Duchess of Milan. The portrait of Christina by Hans Holbein reveals a plump-faced girl with full lips, brown eyes and a straight, shapely nose. The English ambassador, who saw Christina in 1538, remarked that she resembled Mary Shelton in appearance and gave a good description of the young duchess. Her complexion was not "pure white", but she had "a singular good countenance", and when she smiled there appeared two dimples in her cheeks and one in her chin. She was "very tall" and her face was described as "gentle".[9] Interestingly, the sketch allegedly depicting Mary Shelton drawn by Hans Holbein presents a person with no similarities to Christina. The subject is an oval-faced young woman with a pointed chin, wide, thin lips and a distinguished nose. The identity of the sitter is based on the inscription in the right upper corner, "The Lady Henegham", as Mary Shelton had married Anthony Heveningham sometime around 1546.

How reliable is this inscription? Holbein did not inscribe the drawings himself. Many of the identifications were provided by John Cheke, a royal tutor, who knew some of the portrayed people. His labels, however, were often incorrect, as demonstrated by recent research.[10] Many inscriptions on Holbein's drawings are in eighteenth-century lettering and should be regarded with scepticism. The sketch of "Lady Henegham", as is the case with many other drawings, offers virtually no clues as to the sitter's identity; there are no initials, no lettered jewellery and no coat of arms. Considering that Mary Shelton resembled the Duchess of Milan, and the sitter of Holbein's sketch allegedly depicting Mary bears no resemblance to her whatsoever, it is highly doubtful that the sitter depicted is Mary Shelton.

It is possible that Mary Shelton's appearance was not the only attribute that drew Henry VIII's attention. The King enjoyed the company of cultured women who shared his interests in poetry, music and dance. One of his early mistresses, Bessie Blount, was highly proficient "in singing, dancing and in all goodly pastimes".[11] Mary's proficiency in poetry certainly distinguished her among other ladies and provided a common ground with the King. Poetry written by women was a rarity in the Tudor period, so Mary Shelton's accomplishments were certainly appreciated by the King, who also composed poems and deemed himself an expert in this department. Henry VIII was used to everyone applauding his skills in poetry, and he took it as a great offence when Anne Boleyn and her brother laughed at "certain ballads" he composed.[12]

The King was not the only man who appreciated Mary's charms, as she was romantically linked to two other men at court. Henry Norris, Henry VIII's Groom of the Stool and a prominent member of the Privy Chamber, decided to seek her hand in marriage, although when exactly their relationship started remains a mystery. The relationship was apparently public knowledge since Norris was visiting the Queen's chambers to pursue Mary honourably, in the presence of other women who acted as chaperones. Neither Mary nor Henry Norris, however, could have predicted that one of these visits would have a disastrous effect on their lives.

NOTES

[1] *Letters and Papers*, Volume 8, n. 263.

[2] In her testament written on 19 December 1556, Lady Anne Shelton mentioned six children: Amy, Elizabeth, Gabrielle, John, Ralph and Thomas. Mary and Margaret were not mentioned. The exact date of Margaret's death remains uncertain, and it is possible that she was dead by then. Amy, Elizabeth and Gabrielle were unmarried, and it seems likely that Anne Shelton mentioned them because they were not as financially secure as Mary was at the time her mother wrote her last will. Harvey, *The Visitation of Norfolk in the Year 1563, Volume 2*, p. 398.

[3] Remley, *Mary Shelton and Her Tudor Literary Millieu*, p. 47.

[4] Ibid., p. 42.

[5] *Letters and Papers*, Volume 7, n. 5.

[6] Latymer, *Cronickille of Anne Bulleyne*, Volume 39 of Camden Fourth Series,, p. 48.

[7] Hart, *Mistresses of Henry VIII*, p. 124.

[8] Remley, op.cit., p. 50.

[9] *Letters and Papers*, Volume 12 Part 2, n. 1187 - 1188.

[10] Ives, *The Life and Death of Anne Boleyn*, p. 41.

[11] Evans, *Ladies-in-Waiting*, p. 25.

[12] *Letters and Papers*, Volume 10, n. 908.

Chapter 8:
1536, THE YEAR OF CHANGE, BEGINS

Sir Henry Norris was frequenting the Queen's chambers so often that some people, like young Francis Weston, who also tarried there quite a bit, suspected that he wasn't only paying court to Mary Shelton. Weston, who enjoyed the company of Anne Boleyn's ladies-in-waiting, told the Queen that "Norris came more unto her chamber for her than for Mistress Shelton".

Norris was due to marry Mary Shelton, but it seems that neither of them was fully committed to their relationship. Norris was hesitant, and Mary was wooed by Weston, or at least this is what Anne Boleyn believed when she berated Weston "because he did love her kinswoman Mrs Shelton and . . . she said he loves not his wife". Weston, who apparently enjoyed the game of courtly love and was a popular man at court, replied that there was one woman in the Queen's household whom he loved better than either Mary Shelton or his wife. When Anne Boleyn asked who this woman was, Weston playfully replied that it was Anne herself, but she rebuked him.

Weston's information about Norris made Anne Boleyn uneasy, so she decided to confront Norris and asked him "why he went not through with his marriage?" Norris replied that he would "tarry a time"—that is, he would wait. It was not the kind of response Anne Boleyn wanted to hear and so she boldly replied that "you look for a dead man's shoes, for if aught came to the King but good, you would look to have me." The conversation was dangerously spinning out of control, and Norris replied that if he had any such thought, he would deserve to have his head cut off. Then Anne mischievously replied that she could "undo him" if she so wished, and a quarrel ensued between them.

Anne Boleyn's political enemies were quick to build heavy innuendo on this incident, and the Queen was moved to take her little daughter in her arms in the gardens at Greenwich Palace and hold her up to the King as he looked down on them from an open window. The gestures and words the royal couple exchanged that day were dramatic, although the person who later reported this unusual scene was not close enough to hear what was being said. Several days later, one of the leaders of the anti-Boleyn faction was heard saying that Anne Boleyn would soon be dismissed because the King "could not bear her any longer".[1]

Indeed, the Queen had every reason to be worried. Although her long-time rival, Katherine of Aragon, had died in early January of 1536, Anne miscarried a son at the end of the month. Anne herself blamed Mary Howard's father for the miscarriage, claiming that he had unceremoniously informed her about Henry VIII's dangerous fall from a horse during a joust on 24 January. According to the imperial ambassador, Mary Shelton, her mother and sisters "greatly mourned" over Anne's miscarriage, fearing that the King would take another wife.[2]

They had every reason to fear because wild gossip had broken over the court. Some people speculated that Anne Boleyn's "defective constitution" rendered her incapable of bearing male children. Others heard that Henry VIII was thinking about repudiating Anne, as he believed that he "had been seduced and forced into this second marriage by witchcraft".[3] It was plain for all to see that the King was disillusioned with what he perceived as Anne Boleyn's failure, and he started courting one of her maids of honour, Jane Seymour.

Apart from the Duke of Norfolk, Anne also blamed Henry VIII and his new amour for losing a son. She strongly disliked Jane Seymour and "there was much scratching and bye blows between the Queen and her maid".[4] The Queen apparently felt that something was wrong because in April 1536 she entrusted her daughter's spiritual well-being to one of her chaplains, Matthew Parker. What happened next took everyone by surprise.

The May Day joust of 1 May 1536 went ahead as planned. At this point only the King and his councillors knew that Mark Smeaton, the courtly musician, had been arrested and interrogated. Anne Boleyn later recalled that:

"I never spoke with him since but upon Saturday before May Day, and then I found him standing in the round window in my chamber of presence; and I asked why he was so sad, and he answered and said it was no matter. And then I said, 'You may not look to have me speak to you as I should do to a noble man because you are an inferior person.' 'No, no said he, 'a look sufficed me; and thus fare you well'."[5]

This conversation was also reported to the authorities, and this is why Smeaton was arrested. The musician admitted that he had known Anne carnally, but there is a hint that his confession may have been extracted with torture. George Constantine, Henry Norris's servant, said that it was rumoured that Smeaton was "grievously racked" but admitted that he did not know whether it was true or not.[6] Perhaps Anne Boleyn and her circle noticed the musician's absence, or perhaps they were so engrossed in the festivities that they did not notice him gone. The May Day joust was, by all accounts, a magnificent affair. Henry Norris and George Boleyn took part in it, but Henry VIII was confined to the role of spectator since he had suffered a dangerous fall from his horse during the winter tournament, which left him unconscious for two hours. This accident crippled one of Henry's legs and marked the beginning of serious health problems for him.

Towards the end of the joust, Henry VIII suddenly rose and left Greenwich on horseback with only six attendants. Chronicler Edward Hall wrote that "at this sudden departing many men mused, but most chiefly the Queen".[7] Later, hostile sources claimed that the King departed in such haste because he saw Anne Boleyn "who was at a window looking on, drop her handkerchief, that one of her lovers might wipe his face running with sweat".[8]

Whatever the cause of his sudden leaving, the King took Henry Norris with him. Norris had no reasons to fear, as the King was very gracious towards him during the tournament, presenting him with his own mount when Norris's horse stumbled. But the pleasant ride to Whitehall turned into an interrogation when Henry VIII started questioning Henry Norris about his relationship with Anne Boleyn. Norris's servant later confessed that "the King had Mr Norris in examination and promised him his pardon in case he would utter the truth. But whatsoever could be said or done, Mr Norris would confess nothing to the King."[9] He was held in Whitehall Palace overnight and taken to the Tower the next morning.

It seems that the arrest weakened Norris's resolve and he confessed something, but later he withdrew his confession and claimed that he was "deceived" by William FitzWilliam.[10] The question of why Henry VIII decided to examine Norris himself has never been satisfactorily answered. If the King engineered Anne Boleyn's fall, he had no reason to interrogate anyone as he was well aware that charges against Anne and the men accused as her lovers were false. The only explanation of Norris's interrogation may be that Henry VIII believed in Anne's guilt and presumed that Norris was her lover.

Anne's unfortunate comment about "dead man's shoes" had certainly added to the King's suspicions, but there is one more aspect of this matter hitherto unnoticed by historians. Norris courted Mary Shelton, Henry VIII's former mistress. It is well known that the King arranged marriages for his unmarried mistresses when he set them aside. Two of Henry VIII's lovers, Bessie Blount and Margaret Skipwith, were married off as soon as their relationship with the King ended. When Leonard Grey pursued the widowed Bessie Blount in 1532, he was eager to learn if the King was not displeased. Similar approach was taken by Peter Carew when he courted Margaret Skipwith; he even asked if the King could intervene on his behalf with the lady. Upon appreciating Carew's "worthiness and nobility", Henry VIII wrote "his most earnest letters unto the lady in his behalf, and promised also to give with that marriage a hundred pound land to them and to the heirs of their bodies".[11] These two examples clearly show that there existed an unwritten rule of seeking the King's permission for pursuing his former mistress. Did Henry Norris ask the King if he could pursue Mary Shelton? There is no evidence that he did. In fact, Anne Boleyn's comment that Norris wanted to marry her if anything bad happened to the King, coupled with Norris's courtship of Mary Shelton, may have aroused the King's suspicion; if Norris dared to reach for Henry VIII's former mistress, why not seduce his own wife, the Queen?

On 2 May 1536, Anne Boleyn was accused of adultery with five men of Henry VIII's privy chamber, including Henry Norris and Francis Weston. To spice up the indictment and further humiliate the Queen, she was also accused of incest with her brother. Henry VIII's secretary, a man usually blamed for engineering Anne's fall, Thomas Cromwell, would later claim that ladies-in-waiting accused their Queen because they could contain her immoral behaviour no longer. But is it possible that Anne Boleyn could have committed multiple counts of adultery and incest while surrounded by her women on a daily basis? George Wyatt, who wrote an early biography of Anne Boleyn, believed that it was virtually impossible because Anne could not "remove so great ladies, by office appointed to attend on her continually".[12] Another source claimed that Anne's serving women were offered bribes to testify against her. Some had apparently succumbed and provided false evidence.

Mary Howard's father, the Duke of Norfolk, was among the members of Henry VIII's council who came to arrest the Queen and convey her to the Tower by barge. The Queen later recalled how Norfolk said, "tut, tut, tut . . .

shaking his head three or four times" in an attempt to admonish Anne and distance himself from his disgraced niece. Norfolk played a prominent part in Anne Boleyn's fall because he held the office of Lord High Steward and presided over the trials of Norris, Brereton, Weston and Smeaton as well as George Boleyn and the Queen herself. Norfolk's eldest son and Mary's brother, the Earl of Surrey, was present at the trials as The Earl Marshal of England.

It seems, however, that the Howard men were genuinely surprised by the unfolding events of May 1536. The Boleyn Queen's fall paved the way for the Seymour ascendancy, and the Howards would, in the near future, detest the Seymours as ambitious social climbers. Despite the fact that Anne Boleyn professed her innocence throughout her incarceration in the Tower and during her trial, she was nevertheless sentenced to death by twenty-six peers of the realm, including Mary Howard's husband, Henry Fitzroy. When Norfolk read out the verdict, "thou shalt be burned here within the Tower of London, on the Green, else to have thy head smitten off, as the King's pleasure shall be further known of the same", a stream of tears poured down his wrinkled face. The people who filled the courtroom were astounded to see Anne Boleyn composed until the end of her trial. She defended herself eloquently and said she was sorry that five innocent men would lose their lives on her account. As for herself, she added boldly that she was not afraid to die. Then she left the courtroom and was escorted to her royal apartments in the Tower.

Where did Margaret Douglas, Mary Howard and Mary Shelton fit into all of this? There are some tantalising pieces of evidence that are shedding light on their opinions about the Queen. Nicola Shulman, author of a recent biography of Thomas Wyatt, was first to point out that the *Devonshire Manuscript* contains transcribed verses of one of Thomas Wyatt's poems: "I was made a filling instrument/to frame other, while I was beguiled".[13] Wyatt had been briefly imprisoned under suspicion of being one of the Queen's paramours, but he was later released. Shulman proposed that Wyatt cooperated with the authorities, providing some details about Anne Boleyn's circle. He was rewarded with £100 in May 1536, a date implicating he may have been interrogated and coerced into providing damning details. Wyatt's poem suggests that he felt ill-used or perhaps even forced to confess certain things about Anne and five condemned men.[14] The fact that this particular sonnet was circulating among the Devonshire group—a group strongly connected to Anne Boleyn and men who were executed as her "lovers"—suggests that people who transcribed the verses, including Margaret Douglas, Mary Howard and Mary Shelton, went through similar ordeals.

For instance, we know for certain that one of Anne Boleyn's maids of honour, Margery Horsman, was reluctant to cooperate with the authorities and provide damning details about Anne because "there has lately been great friendship between the Queen and her".[15] There is no doubt that other members of Anne's household had been interrogated because Cromwell mentioned this fact in his letters. The Countess of Worcester, for instance, was named as the Queen's "first accuser", although she and Anne Boleyn were close friends, or at least this is what the Queen believed when she "much lamented my Lady of Worcester" because "her child did not stir in her body . . . for the sorrow she took for me". It was the Countess of Worcester who, according to a poem written shortly after Anne Boleyn's execution, claimed that the Queen shared a sexual relationship with her brother, George, and the courtly musician, Mark Smeaton. It was, however, revealed by accident when the countess's brother berated her for loose morals. Defending herself, the countess accused Anne Boleyn of being morally lax. During Anne's trial, however, the imperial ambassador remarked that "no witnesses were called to give evidence . . . as is customary in such cases when the accused denies the charge brought against him". Chapuys, who was also a lawyer, knew that this was highly unusual and suspicious.

Anne Boleyn was executed as an adulteress on 19 May 1536. Four women accompanied her to the scaffold, but history failed to record their names. While she was imprisoned, Anne complained that Henry VIII appointed such servants about her as she never loved and expressed the desire to have her trusted ladies with her. Did Henry VIII take pity on his wife and allow her to pick four attendants from among the ladies of her Privy Chamber? It may be so since the women who accompanied Anne in the Tower were middle-aged, and one of the eyewitness reports says clearly that the four women who escorted Anne to the scaffold and helped her prepare before the swordsman's blow were "young".[16] We may only guess if any of our heroines were among them. They were all either in their teens, like the seventeen-year-old Mary Howard, or in their early twenties, like the twenty-one-year-old Margaret Douglas, so they certainly fit the description. They all stood highly in the Queen's favour and accompanied her at major events in her life. It remains an open possibility that they have also accompanied her in death.

Despite everything that happened in May 1536, Mary Howard retained a good opinion of her royal mistress. She embraced the New Religion and became a renowned patroness of evangelicals. Perhaps her early religious views were shaped by Anne Boleyn's religious tendencies? She sheltered the famous John Foxe, who would become known for his *Actes and Monuments* (*Book of Martyrs*), and provided valuable information about Anne Boleyn's charitable work. Foxe was meticulous when it came to including sources of his information, and when he wrote about Anne Boleyn's "liberal and bountiful distribution to the poor", he made sure to emphasize that he knew about it from "divers credible persons who were about this Queen, and daily acquainted with her doings. . . specially the Duchess of Richmond by name."[17] Mary recalled that Anne always carried a purse of money with her, and whenever she met poor people, she would distribute alms to help them. Although Anne Boleyn was an executed adulteress, the image that stuck in Mary Howard's head was that of a pious, charitable and kind woman who used her influence to help those less fortunate. This fact certainly speaks volumes of what Mary Howard thought about Anne Boleyn and what kind of memories she kept alive. She certainly took to heart the Queen's last words: "And if any person will meddle of my cause, I require them to judge the best".

NOTES

[1] *Calendar of State Papers, Spain,* Volume 5 Part 2, n. 47.
[2] Ibid., n. 21.
[3] Ibid., n. 13.
[4] Clifford, *The Life of Jane Dormer, Duchess of Feria,* p. 41
[5] *Letters and Papers,* Volume 10, n. 798.
[6] *A Memorial from George Constantine to Thomas Lord Cromwell,* p. 205.
[7] *Hall's Chronicle,* p. 819.
[8] Sander, *The Rise and Growth of Anglican Schism,* p. 133.
[9] *A Memorial from George Constantine to Thomas Lord Cromwell,* p.206.
[10] Ibid.
[11] Norton, *Bessie Blount,* p. 295.
[12] Wyatt, *The Life of Anne Boleigne,* p. 211.
[13] Shulman, *Graven with Diamonds,* p. 195.
[14] Ibid., p. 197.
[15] *Letters and Papers,* Volume 10, n. 799.
[16] Ibid. n. 911.
[17] Foxe, *Book of Martyrs: The Actes and Monuments of the Church,* Volume 2, p. 372.

CHAPTER 9:
IN THE SHADOW OF THE TOWER

The court turned its back on the bloody events of May 1536. Only the heartbroken poet Thomas Wyatt seemed to remember the victims of one of the most spectacular and violent coups in the history of England: "These bloody days have broken my heart . . . my lust, my youth did them depart". Many men and women certainly shared Wyatt's pain, but they had to move on with their lives as everyone around them did. Henry VIII quickly forgot about his executed wife, whose truncated body was laid to rest in an arrow chest in the little chapel of St Peter ad Vincula, and married his third wife, Jane Seymour, only eleven days after Anne Boleyn's death.

On 15 June 1536, Corpus Christi Day, Henry VIII made a public demonstration of his new marriage and went in procession with Jane Seymour from Whitehall Palace to Westminster Abbey. The new Queen was attended by her predecessor's maids of honour and ladies-in-waiting, including Margaret Douglas, who was carrying the long train of Jane Seymour's gown.[1] The festivities continued until the end of the month, but in early July the atmosphere of joy was shattered when two dramatic events occurred. First, Henry VIII's illegitimate son, Henry Fitzroy, fell mortally ill. Second, the King learned that his niece had secretly married Lord Thomas Howard, Mary Howard's half uncle.

The young Lord Howard, born about 1512, was only three years older than Margaret Douglas. Nothing is known about his appearance or personal attributes apart from the fact that he was closely associated with the Devonshire group. If Margaret and Thomas believed that Henry VIII would smile on their union, they were terribly mistaken. At this point, Henry VIII was paranoid about the succession. According to the preamble to the statute by which Princess Elizabeth, Henry's daughter by Anne Boleyn, was bastardised and subsequently disinherited, Anne confessed to Archbishop Cranmer that there were some "just, true and lawful impediments" to her marriage with the King.[2] Thanks to this confession, by June 1536 all of Henry VIII's children, including Lady Mary, who was forced to sign a document admitting that her parents' marriage was unlawful, were declared illegitimate and thus unfit to inherit the throne.

The King's hopes for the succession now rested on his illegitimate son's shoulders. The imperial ambassador Chapuys reported in early June that Robert Radcliffe, Earl of Sussex, "stated the other day in the Privy Council in the King's presence that, considering the Princess [Mary Tudor] as a bastard, as well as the Duke of Richmond [Henry Fitzroy], it was advisable to prefer the male to the female for the succession to the crown".[3] For the first time since Fitzroy's birth, Henry VIII's illegitimate son became a serious contender for the throne. In the summer of 1536, it was evident that until Jane Seymour bore sons, the succession crisis had to be sorted out. In July, parliament passed an act which did not confine the succession to legitimate heirs but allowed Henry VIII to choose whomever he wished as his successor. "If such person", the act stated, "should be so named, [they] might happen to take great heart and courage, and by presumption fall into disobedience and rebellion".[4] It is obvious that Henry VIII had opened up the possibility that in case of a lack of legitimate male heirs, his crown would be inherited by Fitzroy.

Mary Howard's feelings about her husband's eventual inheritance of the throne are unknown. What is certain is that in the summer of 1536, Mary could have hoped to become Queen consort one day, especially because the King was heard saying that Jane Seymour was unable to bear him sons. Unfortunately, this hope would last only for a brief spell, as Fitzroy's health began to deteriorate.

The ever vigilant imperial ambassador reported that Henry VIII was mortified with Margaret Douglas's secret marriage to Lord Howard because he was aware that Fitzroy "could not live long", and he had intended to make him his successor. Now, when his illegitimate son lay dying at St James's Palace, Henry VIII was left with two illegitimate daughters and no sons. Margaret Douglas, legitimate princess of the blood, suddenly became a very important person and a possible heiress to the throne.

The King convinced himself that Lord Thomas Howard was aiming for his crown. It must have dawned on Henry that he was surrounded by the ambitious Howards; his executed wife was one of them, and she had managed to assimilate the King's son into their ranks. Now, yet another Howard had married into the royal family. On 8 July 1536, Margaret Douglas and Lord Howard were imprisoned in the Tower of London. That same day, the imperial ambassador reported that Mary Howard's husband had been "in a state of rapid consumption" and, according to his physicians, he could not live many more months.[5]

The nature of the promises exchanged by Margaret Douglas and Lord Howard must be tackled. According to Catholic canon law—still applicable at the time—a marriage contract was valid when made "de presenti", wherein the couple verbally claimed each other in the present tense. If such a pledge was followed by sexual intercourse, the marriage contract was indissoluble. According to the imperial ambassador, Margaret and Thomas were contracted "de presenti" to wed, but they did not consummate their marriage.[6]

Lord Thomas Howard, as well as the former members of Anne Boleyn's household, was questioned on 9 July 1536. According to Lord Howard, he had known Margaret Douglas for about a year when they pledged their troth on 16 April 1536. They also exchanged gifts: he gave her a cramp ring to ward off sickness, and she presented him with her painted miniature and a diamond. In the examination of one Thomas Smith in relation to this matter, he confessed that Lord Howard would wait until Lady Boleyn, one of Anne Boleyn's aunts, was gone from Margaret Douglas's chamber, leaving only Mary Howard to attend Margaret before Lord Howard would enter. When

Lord Howard was asked who knew about their secret marriage, he replied that Margaret told his brother's wife, and he confided to one of his mother's servants. It is obvious that Lord Howard sought to protect the members of his family. The deposition of Thomas Smith makes it clear that some women close to Margaret Douglas knew about the marriage as well, although he did not provide names.[7]

Mary Howard, Margaret's friend and confidante, who acted as a chaperone for the two lovers, was most probably privy to this secret, but she was neither questioned nor sent to the Tower. She was spared the examination because her husband, Henry Fitzroy, was dying. On 18 July, it was common knowledge at court that "my Lord of Richmond is very sick".[8] Five days later, he was dead.[9]

Meanwhile, in the Tower, Margaret Douglas and Lord Howard continued to scribble love notes to each other: Howard called her "mine own sweet wife", and she responded in equally warm terms. Although their bodies suffered, one lyrical note claimed their hearts "shall be of one estate". These and many other touching notes were transcribed by Mary Shelton and preserved in the *Devonshire Manuscript*.

There is only one question: How could Margaret Douglas and Lord Howard exchange love notes if they were imprisoned separately? It seems that the couple was able to communicate thanks to Mary Shelton's brother, Thomas, who was a groom porter in the Tower of London.[10] The King, unfortunately, did not share their enthusiasm for the match. Although marrying a member of the royal family was not a treasonous act in itself, Lord Howard was condemned by an act of attainder; he was declared a traitor by statute and not by trial. The act stated that:

"Lord Thomas Howard, brother to Thomas now Duke of Norfolk, being led and seduced by the devil, not having God afore his eyes, nor regarding his duty of allegiance that he owed to have borne to the King, our and his most dread sovereign lord, had now lately, within the King's own court and mansion place at Westminster . . . without the knowledge or assent of our said most dread sovereign lord the King, contemptuously and traitorously contracted himself, by crafty, fair, and flattering words, to and with the Lady Margaret Douglas, being natural daughter of the Queen of Scots, elder sister to our said sovereign lord."[11]

Margaret Douglas's mother, the Dowager Queen of Scots, was horrified to learn about her daughter's imprisonment, and on 12 August 1536 she penned a touching letter to her royal brother, pleading for her daughter's life:

"Dearest brother, we beseech Your Grace, of sisterly kindness and natural love we bear, and that you owe to us, your only sister, to have compassion and pity of us, your sister, and of our natural daughter and sister to the King, our only natural son and your dearest nephew [James V of Scotland]; and to grant our said daughter Margaret Your Grace's pardon, grace and favour, and remit of such as Your Grace has put to her charge."[12]

The Dowager Queen of Scots was aware that at this point her daughter could end up at the scaffold, considering that only three months earlier Henry VIII had not hesitated to execute his own wife. She proposed to have Margaret sent back to Scotland so that "in time coming she shall never come in Your Grace's presence".[13] But Margaret Douglas was too valuable a pawn to be executed or banished. The imperial ambassador Chapuys believed that Margaret would not be punished because her marriage was not consummated, and even if it was, "she still deserved forgiveness; for, after all, she has witnessed and is daily witnessing many examples of that in her own domestic circle."[14] However, Lord Howard deserved, in the King's perception, to be sentenced to death because, as the act against him stated, he:

". . . hath imagined and compassed, that in case our said sovereign lord should die without heirs of his body, which God defend, that then the said Lord Thomas, by reason of marriage in so high a blood . . . should aspire by her [Margaret Douglas] to the dignity of the said imperial crown of this realm . . ."

Henry VIII's growing fears and paranoia are clearly visible here. It is doubtful that in April 1536, when Margaret and Thomas contracted a secret marriage, the couple harboured malicious intentions. The King was, at the time, married to Anne Boleyn and had a legitimate daughter by her. It was not until July 1536, when both Henry VIII's daughters were declared illegitimate and Henry Fitzroy fell mortally ill, that the circumstances had changed dramatically for Margaret Douglas and Lord Howard. There was no "traitorous intent" on Lord Howard's part; it seems that he had genuinely fallen in love with Margaret. Unfortunately, he chose the wrong time to pledge himself to her and incurred the King's wrath.

Although languishing in the Tower, Margaret Douglas was lodged comfortably. As an aristocrat and the

King's niece, she was placed in luxurious conditions. In December, for instance, her chairs were upholstered with crimson velvet, and silver fringe was provided for her use. She was also served by several members of her own household but angered the King by admitting some of Lord Howard's servants. In her letter to Thomas Cromwell, she assured him that she only did it because they were poor. The King was displeased because Margaret seemed to signal that she still entertained hopes to be reunited with her husband and pardoned. She realised that it was a mistake and wrote to Cromwell:

"But seeing, my lord, that it is your pleasure that I shall keep none that did belong unto my Lord Thomas, I will put them from me. And I beseech you not to think that any fancy doth remain in me touching him; but that all my study and care is how to please the King's Grace, and to continue in his favour."[15]

Margaret's assurance that she did not harbour romantic feelings towards Lord Howard was probably her attempt to save him from the executioner's blade. But she did care for him, and the thought of his impending death grieved her sorely. Margaret's health began to deteriorate, and various medicaments were prescribed "for the relief and conservation" of her health "during the time of her being in the Tower of London and also since the same".[16] It was probably the poor state of Margaret's health that prompted Henry VIII to move her from within the imposing walls of the Tower to Syon Abbey, where she was kept under house arrest.[17]

Lord Thomas Howard was not so lucky; although his life was spared, he never left the Tower of London and died there on 31 October 1537 of what one of his contemporaries described as an "ague".[18] Margaret, according to *Wriothesley's Chronicle*, "took his death very heavily".[19] She was released from house arrest shortly after Lord Howard's death and attended Queen Jane Seymour's funeral on 12 November 1537.[20] Thomas was buried without pomp in his family's vault at Thetford priory later that month. His unjust and untimely death provoked a strong reaction from other members of the Devonshire group. Their feelings are reflected in a poem written by Mary Howard's brother, the Earl of Surrey. "For you yourself have heard, it is not long ago, since that for love one of the race did end his life in woe." The "race" in this instance refers to the Howard dynasty. The poem goes on to say that Lord Howard spent his last days in tears and died "for loss of his true love".[21] It was a silent protest against the injustice done to one of the Howards.

NOTES

[1] *Wriothesley's Chronicle,* Volume 1, p. 48.

[2] Strype, *Memorials of Archbishop Cranmer,* Volume 1, p. 101.

[3] *Calendar of State Papers, Spain,* Volume 5 Part 2, n. 61.

[4] Lipscomb, *1536: The Year that Changed Henry VIII,* p. 93.

[5] *Calendar of State Papers, Spain,* Volume 5 Part 2, n. 71.

[6] *Letters and Papers, Volume 11,* n. 147.

[7] Ibid., n. 48.

[8] Ibid., n. 108.

[9] Wriothesley in his chronicle stated that Fitzroy died on 22 July 1536, while Chapuys reported that he died in the morning of 23 July.

[10] Remley, *Mary Shelton and Her Tudor Literary Milieu,* p. 54.

[11] Everett-Wood, *Letters of Royal and Illustrious Ladies,* Volume 2, p. 285.

[12] Ibid., p. 287.

[13] Ibid., p. 288.

[14] *Calendar of State Papers, Spain,* Volume 5 Part 2, n. 77.

[15] Everett-Wood, op.cit., pp. 292-3.

[16] St Clare Byrne, *The Lisle Letters,* Volume 3, p. 459.

[17] Despite the fact that chronicles of Wriothesley and Holinshed state that Margaret Douglas was not released from the Tower until October 1537, the letter from the Abess of Syon written to Thomas Cromwell on 6 November 1536 makes it clear that Margaret was lodged there in the autumn of 1536. *Letters and Papers (Henry VIII),* Volume 11, n. 994.

[18] St Clare Byrne, *The Lisle Letters,* Volume 4, p. 179.

[19] *Wriothesley's Chronicle,* Volume 1, p. 70.

[20] *Letters and Papers,* Volume 12 part 2, n. 1060.

[21] Childs, *Henry VIII's Last Victim,* p. 113.

CHAPTER 10:
"THE POOREST WIDOW OF THE REALM"

It is generally accepted that Mary Howard's husband, Henry Fitzroy, was killed by tuberculosis. He was slowly wasting away, but for some reason, his contemporaries assumed foul play. *Wriothesley's Chronicle* recorded that "it was thought that he was privily poisoned by the means of Queen Anne and her brother, Lord Rochford, for he pined inwardly in his body long before he died."[1]

On the day of Anne Boleyn's arrest, when Fitzroy had come to the King to wish him good night, Henry VIII began to weep and made a shocking confession to his son. He told Fitzroy that he and his half sister, Mary, "owed God a great debt" because Anne Boleyn, whom the King dubbed "that accursed whore", had tried to poison them.[2]

According to the imperial ambassador, during her trial Anne stood accused of poisoning Katherine of Aragon and attempting to do the same with the King's elder daughter. It was well known at court that Anne wanted to see her rivals dead and boasted on several occasions that she could undo them using poison if she so wished. The Queen, however, was known to have had a volatile temper and quick tongue, and though she did not poison anyone, people were ready to believe the worst of her.

Henry Fitzroy, who attended Anne Boleyn's execution, may well have been convinced that she had indeed tried to poison him, especially when he learned about it from his royal father. Perhaps the King believed these rumours himself or, what seems most likely, had convinced himself that they were true.

After Henry Fitzroy's death, it was common knowledge at court that "he had never lain by his wife, and so she is maid, wife, and now a widow."[3] Considering the fact that Fitzroy's physicians believed he would not live long, Mary Howard might have been prepared for the worst, but who informed her of Fitzroy's death and how she reacted to the news remains unknown. In one of her letters, Mary confessed that Fitzroy's death caused her "sorrow and discomfort", but this is her only statement concerning her husband's death.[4] Mary's brother, Surrey, who was raised with Fitzroy, grieved his brother-in-law's death and experienced annual bouts of melancholy whenever he "thought of my Lord of Richmond".[5] It remains unknown whether Mary felt the same.

Henry VIII reacted to his son's death with a mixture of grief and denial. Mary's father, the Duke of Norfolk, asked the King for permission to bury Fitzroy among his Howard ancestors in Thetford Priory. Henry VIII granted the permission and requested a humble, almost secretive funeral. Norfolk would later recall: "The King's pleasure was that his body should be conveyed secretly in a closed cart."[6] In early August, the imperial ambassador reported that Fitzroy's body "has been secretly carried in a wagon covered with straw, without any company except two persons clothed in green, who followed at a distance, into Norfolk, where the duke, his father-in-law, will have him buried."[7]

Two days after this report, Norfolk heard that Henry VIII was displeased with him "because my Lord of Richmond was not buried honourably".[8] Norfolk admitted that he had allowed more pomp than the King himself initially planned. Henry Fitzroy's body was wrapped in lead and a closed cart was provided, but it was not conveyed secretly. Norfolk must have been stunned when he learned that rumour had it that Henry VIII planned to send him to the Tower. Prompted by fear, Norfolk sat down to write his last will. In the end, however, he was not sent to languish in the Tower, but he and his son remained in the King's disfavour.

Mary Howard was also about to experience the King's capricious nature because he, unlike Mary and her kin, believed that Fitzroy was never married to her because their marriage was not consummated. The Duke of Norfolk, Mary's father, decided to seek Thomas Cromwell's help to remedy this situation. In October 1536, he wrote a letter detailing the circumstances of his daughter's marriage. Norfolk claimed that Henry VIII was solely responsible for arranging the match: "the marriage was made by his commandment, without that I ever made suit thereof".[9]

Mary's mother, the proud Duchess of Norfolk, was of a very different opinion: "Queen Anne got the marriage [with Fitzroy] clear for my lord my husband, when she did favour my lord my husband".[10] The fact that Henry VIII sought to distance himself from the Howards strongly implies that it was indeed Anne Boleyn who promoted the match between Mary Howard and Henry Fitzroy. And Anne Boleyn, according to the duchess, made grand promises about Mary's jointure:

"I heard Queen Anne say that if my Lord of Richmond did die, that my daughter should have above a thousand pounds a year to her jointure."[11]

But Henry VIII would hear none of it. The Duke of Norfolk, who was preparing to depart north to quell a religious rebellion known as the Pilgrimage of Grace in October 1536, was eager to keep his "daughter's cause" open for negotiations:

"Good my lord, help, that the matter may soon take effect; for I would not be a little sorry to depart to dwell in the north, and to leave her behind me, for I am somewhat jealous of her that, being out of my company, she might bestow herself otherwise than I would she should; notwithstanding that, unto this time, it is not possible for a young woman to handle herself more discreetly than she hath done since her husband's death".[12]

Mary's well-being was very much in Norfolk's heart, and shortly before his departure, he begged Henry VIII to "be good to my sons and to my poor daughter".[13] The King declared that he would look after Norfolk's children, the duke's "lively images".[14] During his mission in the north, Norfolk almost fell into disgrace when he made some unauthorised promises to the rebels. Norfolk's enemies at court used his absence to their advantage and spread rumours that Norfolk sympathised with the rebels because he himself was a staunch Catholic. The King, always prone to manipulation, wrote Norfolk an angry letter, accusing him of inaction and negligence. Norfolk knew there was no other option to redeem himself in the King's eyes, and he ordered the merciless executions of the rebels.

But Norfolk's enemies were still bent on his destruction and accused Norfolk's eldest son, Surrey, who joined his father in the north in March 1537, of sympathising with the rebels' cause. Although Norfolk and Surrey eventually avoided the King's wrath, the Pilgrimage of Grace allowed the Howards' enemies to try to hound them out of royal favour. In such circumstances, Mary Howard's case was temporarily forgotten. The events that played out that summer did not help. In July of 1537, while Mary's father still dwelled in the north, her brother returned home and visited court. Ever since Henry Fitzroy's death, Surrey was left without a friend and hated the new men at court. Just recently he had experienced what one historian called "an anniversary reaction" to Henry Fitzroy's death and, considering the nature of accusations against him and his father, his return to court strained him emotionally.[15] Always rash and impetuous, Surrey struck one courtier in the face, presumably after being provoked into a quarrel. The punishment for such a crime was the loss of a right hand. As a poet and a soldier, this was a punishment that would render Surrey incapable of fighting and writing. In the end, however, Surrey's hand was saved, but he was sent to solitary exile at Windsor Castle.

In October 1537, both Surrey and Norfolk were back at court. Queen Jane Seymour gave birth to Prince Edward on 12 October, and the grand christening took place three days later, with Mary's father and brother prominent during the ceremony. On 23 October 1537, Queen Jane died of childbed fever and was buried on 12 November. Mary Howard's presence was not recorded either at the christening of the prince or at the Queen's funeral.

On 19 December 1537, she wrote a letter to her father from Kenninghall, which proves beyond doubt that Mary did not serve as Queen Jane's lady-in-waiting. When exactly she decided to retire from court remains unknown, but it is highly likely that it occurred shortly after her husband's death. The execution of Anne Boleyn, the arrest of Margaret Douglas and Lord Howard, as well as Henry Fitzroy's death probably proved too much to bear for the young girl of seventeen. However, in December 1537, Mary felt strong enough to write to her father and remind him of her suit. She apologised for troubling him with her letters, but she acknowledged that he was "such a good intercessor to the King's Majesty on my behalf" and thus the only person who could help her. However, because there was no effect of her pleas "but words", she expressed her doubt whether the King was informed about her plea. One of the strongest lines of Mary's letter touches the King himself:

"I am sure he would never suffer the justice of his laws to be denied to me, the unworthy desolate widow of his late son that never yet was denied to the poorest gentlewoman in this realm."

She was not afraid to come to court and sue for her cause in person because she believed that the King's heart would be moved "to have compassion on me, considering that he himself alone made the marriage".[16] Here, Mary was perhaps implying that whether the match was Anne Boleyn's brainchild or not, it was the King who had ultimately agreed to it. Norfolk's response was immediate. He met with his daughter at Stoke by Nayland sometime between 19 December 1537 and 8 January 1538 and learned that Mary had taken matters into her own hands. On 8 January 1538, Norfolk penned a letter to Thomas Cromwell, informing him that Mary had been:

". . . put in such comfort by learned men that her right is clearly good, and that she hath been delayed so long (as she thinketh) for lack of good suit made to the King's highness by me; so that on my faith I well perceive she doth think I care little for her cause, and doth not doubt but that by her own suit, her matter being so good as it is, she should soon obtain it at His Majesty's hand".[17]

In other words, Mary consulted the lawyers without her father's consent and had been assured that her right to obtain a jointure from the King was incontestable. Norfolk was certainly surprised, but Mary had done nothing against the royal etiquette. As a widow, she attained the legal status of "feme sole", an independent woman. Mary obviously believed that her father was not diligent enough in her cause, although Norfolk's letters make it clear that his daughter's well-being was always at his heart. Unlike Mary, however, Norfolk sought the right time to approach Henry VIII. This was the first time Norfolk realized how strong and determined a daughter he had:

"My lord, in all my life I never communed [talked] with her in any serious cause until now, and would not have thought she had been such as I find her, which, as I think, is but too wise for a woman".[18]

Norfolk was now reluctant to allow Mary to go to court. Perhaps he feared that such an outspoken and determined woman could only remind Henry VIII about his second wife, Anne Boleyn. What Norfolk did not know was that his daughter had already written a letter to Thomas Cromwell, asking him directly to intercede with the King on her behalf. Her letter is a testament of her strong will and courage:

"My singular good lord,

In mine humble manner I commend me to your good lordship. And where it hath pleased Almighty God to call to his mercy my late lord and husband one year and a half past, to my most sorrow and discomfort; and my lord my father, under whose tuition I am, hath many times promised me to be a suitor to the King's Majesty for obtaining of my dower, whereof as yet there hath no good effect come to me, nor, I fear me, by his means of long time shall not: most humbly and heartily I beseech your good lordship to help me, a desolate widow, that by your good means I may obtain my right, and to be a suitor to His Highness for me for the same.

Of truth, about a fortnight past I wrote a letter to my lord my father, beseeching him to give me licence to come up to sue to His Majesty for mine own cause; whereunto he made me so short an answer, that I am more than half in despair to obtain by his suit. Alas! Good my lord, you that do many deeds, help me, the poorest widow of the realm, and deliver mine humble supplication, which you shall receive with this, to His Highness; and if it may stand with His Highness's pleasure to remit my said cause to the judges and his learned counsel, I am in no doubt they will inform His Majesty that my right is perfect good. There is but one thing, as my counsel say unto me, that doth delay, nor can, my matter, which is, that I cannot have out the writs; wherein, by your good mediation, I trust His Highness will not deny me, which never, unto this time, was denied to any lady or gentlewoman in this realm. Finally, my good lord, most humbly I beseech you to be my good lord concerning the premises, and I shall daily pray to Almighty God for your long prosperity."[19]

The next we hear about Mary Howard is on 6 April 1538, when Norfolk wrote to Cromwell that she "doth continually, with weeping and wailing, cry out on me to have me give her licence to ride to London to sue for her cause, thinking that I have not effectually followed the same." In this letter, Norfolk opened up about why he was reluctant to let Mary go to court:

"My Lord, I am so afraid that the King's Highness should not be content with me to bring her up that, unto this time, for all her pitiful lamenting, I would not grant to her desire."

Knowing that Cromwell was close to the King, Norfolk asked him to "feel His Grace's mind, whether I should displease His Majesty in bringing her up, or not". Norfolk was ready to send his daughter to court with some eighty servants in attendance, but only if Cromwell could assure him that Henry VIII would not be displeased.[20] But the King was not so easily convinced that Mary Howard deserved to receive her jointure, and he would try to stall the negotiations for as long as he possibly could.

NOTES

[1] *Wriothesley's Chronicle*, Volume 1, pp. 53-4.
[2] *Letters and Papers,* Volume 10, n. 908.
[3] *Wriothesley's Chronicle*, Volume 1, p. 54.
[4] Everett-Wood, *Letters of Royal and Illustrious Ladies,*Volume 2, p. 375.
[5] Childs, *Henry VIII's Last Victim*, p. 122.
[6] *Letters and Papers*, Volume 11, n. 233.
[7] Ibid., n. 221.
[8] Ibid., n. 233.
[9] Everett-Wood, op.cit., p. 373.
[10] Ibid. p. 363.
[11] Ibid.
[12] Ibid., p. 374.
[13] Childs, op.cit., p. 117.
[14] Ibid.
[15] Ibid., p. 123.

[16] Henry Ellis, *Original Letters*, 2d series, Volume 2, p. 84.
[17] Everett-Wood, op.cit., pp. 374-75.
[18] Ibid.
[19] Ibid., p. 376.
[20] Ibid., p. 377.

CHAPTER 11:
FAMILY FEUD

Mary Howard's difficulty in obtaining her jointure was not the only problem she had to face after her husband's death. She was dragged into a bitter feud between her parents, who separated in March 1534. Mary's mother, Duchess Elizabeth, never accepted the fact that her husband, the Duke of Norfolk, had taken a mistress. It seems that Norfolk was very fond of Bess Holland, who was considerably younger than him; their relationship lasted for nearly twenty years and did not end until shortly after Norfolk's arrest in 1546. Duchess Elizabeth scorned Bess Holland on the grounds of her lowly status, calling Bess "but a churl's daughter and of no gentle blood" and "a washer in my nursery [for] eight years".[1] Bess's social position was probably not as low as the duchess scornfully asserted, for she was a daughter of the Duke of Norfolk's treasurer and chief steward, John Holland.

Mary Howard's mother was a woman who would not tolerate humiliation easily. She regretted that her husband took up a younger mistress because she herself had been considerably younger when Norfolk married her.

Norfolk chose her to be his wife, although she was already engaged to her father's ward and had younger sisters who were offered instead. "I was of his own choosing", she bitterly bemoaned, "and he not of mine". "He chose me for love and I am younger than he by twenty years", she complained in another letter. It is clear that it was Norfolk's decision to separate from Elizabeth; she admitted that it was he who "put me away".[2]

Husbands took mistresses all the time and, as the experiences of Katherine of Aragon and Anne Boleyn clearly showed, wives were expected to turn a blind eye on such infidelities. Elizabeth, however, would not accept unfaithfulness, ignoring Norfolk's offers of rewards and the return of her jewels and clothes if she agreed to a divorce. She would rather live in solitary confinement than be put to shame.

When the final break between the Norfolks occurred in 1534, Duchess Elizabeth moved to a rented house in Redbourne, Hertfordshire. From there, she penned a series of embittered letters to Thomas Cromwell between 1535 and 1539. In these letters, Elizabeth accused Norfolk and his servants of domestic violence and demanded financial retribution. Duchess Elizabeth claimed that shortly before they separated, Norfolk "came riding all night, and locked me up in a chamber, and took away all my jewels and all my apparel", leaving her only three hundred marks a year to live upon. His servants, the duchess claimed, had bound her, pummelled her and sat on her breast until she "spat blood" only because she dared to speak up against Bess Holland. Duchess Elizabeth referred to her life in Redbourne as "imprisonment" and said that no one dared to visit her except people appointed by Norfolk.

As soon as Elizabeth accepted that she would never live with her husband again, she started petitioning Cromwell to help her obtain a higher income from Norfolk because "I have lived very poorly . . . and not after my bringing up".[3] Among Elizabeth's most shocking claims—uncorroborated by other sources and strenuously denied by Norfolk—were her assertions that when she was in childbed with Mary in 1519, Norfolk had dragged her by her hair out of bed and around the house, wounding her in the head with his dagger. Despite this shocking claim, Mary chose to side with her father.

It is clear that Mary had to support Norfolk, as only he could help her with her jointure. Perhaps Mary, who knew her mother well, suspected—or knew for a fact—that Norfolk had never committed such heinous deeds. In the following excerpt from Norfolk's letter to Thomas

Cromwell, the duke denied that he had ever mistreated his wife in childbed:

"My good lord, if I prove not by witness, and that with many honest persons, that she [his wife] had a scar in her head fifteen months before she was delivered of my said daughter, and that the same was cut by a surgeon of London for a swelling she had in her head of drawing two teeth, never trust my word after; reporting to your good lordship whether I shall play the fool or no, to put me in her danger, that so falsely will slander me, and so wilfully stick thereby. Surely I think there is no man on life that would handle a woman in childbed of that sort, nor for my part would not so have done for all that I am worth."[4]

For Mary, this explanation was enough to believe her father. Mary's brother, Surrey, had also sided with Norfolk, and Duchess Elizabeth was clearly upset with her children, branding them "ungracious", "unkind" and "unnatural". Mary's other brother, Thomas, is not mentioned in the letters, and it is possible that he tried to help his mother out.

Duchess Elizabeth's anger was aimed mainly at her daughter because she formed a close bond with Norfolk's mistress, Bess Holland, and Elizabeth saw this as an ultimate betrayal on Mary's part. When Bess was comfortably installed in her suite of rooms in Kenninghall in 1535, Duchess Elizabeth complained that Mary and Surrey tolerated her presence and called them Norfolk's children rather than her own. She was also highly displeased that Mary went about in Bess's company. It seems that Bess moved in the same social circles as Mary. At some point, perhaps when they all served Anne Boleyn, Bess received a diamond ring from Mary Shelton, one of Mary Howard's close friends.[5]

Such closeness annoyed the duchess, who, upon hearing that Mary's jointure had not yet been granted, asked Thomas Cromwell to ensure that Henry VIII did not pay Mary her allowance until she first received hers. The reason Duchess Elizabeth resorted to such a peculiar request was that she believed her marriage, which had lasted for more than twenty years and produced five children, gave her case precedence over Mary's short-lived, childless union with the King's son.[6] Although she resented the fact that her children supported Norfolk, Elizabeth admitted that she loved them, and there is evidence that Mary eventually met with her mother on at least one more occasion, although it remains unknown whether they were ever reconciled.[7]

NOTES

[1] Everett-Wood, *Letters of Royal and Illustrious Ladies*, Volume 2, pp. 224, 371.
[2] Ibid., p. 367.
[3] Ibid., pp. 361-2.
[4] Ibid., p. 364.
[5] Remley, *Mary Shelton and Her Tudor Literary Milieu*, p. 68.
[6] Everett-Wood, op.cit., p. 363.
[7] Read more in Chapter 16.

CHAPTER 12:
THE KING'S PAWNS

Mary Shelton's feelings about Henry Norris's tragic death are nowhere recorded, and the absence of her name in the court records for the period of Jane Seymour's queenship suggests that she had withdrawn from court after May 1536. This notion is further strengthened by the fact that when Henry VIII's ambassadors were scouring through the European courts in search of a new royal bride for the King after Jane Seymour's death, they informed Thomas Cromwell that Duchess Christina of Milan resembled Mary Shelton, who was referred to as the lady who used to serve in Anne Boleyn's Privy Chamber.[1] Had Mary been Jane Seymour's maid of honour, she would have been certainly referred to as the late Queen's servant.

Mary Shelton's name resurfaced again in January 1538 in a curious letter from John Husee to Lord Arthur Lisle:

"The election lieth betwixt Mistress Mary Shelton and Mistress Mary Skipwith. I pray Jesu send such one as may be for His Highness's comfort and the wealth of the realm. Herein I doubt not but your lordship will keep silence till the matter be surely known."[2]

The fact that this letter was written a month after Henry VIII's ambassador mentioned the resemblance between Mary Shelton and Christina of Milan, before the King decided upon a fourth wife, suggests that Henry VIII was contemplating marrying yet another English lady. The reference to "the wealth of the realm" strongly implies that the widowed King considered one of these ladies as his prospective bride rather than a mistress.

The same letter mentioned that Mary Shelton's uncle, Thomas Boleyn, Earl of Wiltshire, "is again now in the court and very well entertained".[3] It has been recently suggested that Boleyn was back in the royal favour because of the King's affection towards his niece.[4] That may not have been the case, however. Boleyn was an ambitious courtier who had spent his entire life in the royal service. The events of May 1536 clearly show that he abandoned his children and was willing to participate in their trials.[5] At the end of June, he handed the office of Lord Privy Seal to Thomas Cromwell and withdrew from court.

After rusticating in Hever in the summer and early autumn of 1536, he was summoned to quash the Pilgrimage of Grace and was subsequently back in the royal favour, participating in the christening of Prince Edward and the funeral of Queen Jane Seymour in October and November of 1537. By 1538, Thomas Boleyn was back in Henry VIII's good graces. He was apparently much made of at court since the rumour in London in July 1538 had it that "My Lord of Wiltshire should marry with my Lady Margaret Douglas".[6]

Whether it was a mere rumour or an actual possibility contemplated by Henry VIII, we may never know, as contemporaries never returned to this subject again. It seems highly unlikely that Thomas Boleyn, whose wife died in April 1538, would have dared to entertain hope of marrying the King's niece without the royal permission, considering that after Margaret's clandestine marriage to Lord Howard it was considered treason to marry a woman of royal blood without Henry VIII's approval.[7]

If we take Margaret's recent disgrace in connection to her marriage into consideration, it is inconceivable to think that her name would have been linked with anyone if the King was not privy to such plans. The rumours that Thomas Cromwell stood behind Lord Howard's attainder because he wanted to marry Margaret Douglas himself, which emerged during the Pilgrimage of Grace, can easily be dismissed as propaganda spread by the rebels who detested Cromwell's influence and wanted to remove him from power. It is therefore highly possible that the rumour about Thomas Boleyn's marriage to Margaret Douglas was rooted in fact.

Margaret Douglas's thoughts about her prospective Boleyn husband remain unknown, but she couldn't have been thrilled to marry a man thirty-eight years her senior, who gladly returned to court after his children's judicial murders. The plans eventually came to nothing when Thomas Boleyn died the following year, aged 62, and was buried in St. Peter's parish church in Hever.

Meanwhile in July 1538, Thomas Howard, Duke of Norfolk, broached the subject of his daughter's jointure with the King yet again. Despite Mary Howard's fears that her father was not diligent enough in her cause, Norfolk did all that he could to help her. This time, however, Norfolk decided to take things one step further and make "a further overture for the marriage of his said daughter". Mary was now nineteen years old, and her father decided to use her to build a new courtly alliance because his influence was on the wane.

There were two candidates whom Norfolk deemed worthy to become his son-in-law, but one of them was apparently so insignificant that Henry VIII forgot his name. The second candidate, whom Norfolk said was the one "to whom his heart is most inclined", was Thomas Seymour. Although Queen Jane Seymour died shortly after giving birth to Henry VIII's son and heir, Prince Edward, her ambitious brothers, Edward and Thomas, were growing in the King's favour. Norfolk was also quick to grasp that in the event of Henry VIII's death, the Seymour brothers, as uncles to the heir to the throne, would emerge as leading figures in the new regime.

Although Thomas Seymour was suspicious about Norfolk's intentions at first, he eventually accepted the proposal. Marrying a daughter of one of the two remaining dukes was a tempting prospect and one that such an ambitious man as Thomas Seymour found hard to resist. The King was eager to endorse the match between the couple, declaring that Thomas, "one of such lust and youth", would be able to "please" Mary "at all points".[8] Henry VIII was well aware that if Mary Howard remarried, the uncomfortable question of her jointure could finally be forgotten. Perhaps Mary was aware of it as well because the marriage negotiations came to an abrupt end.

In Mary's later words, her "fantasy [fancy] would not serve to marry with" Thomas Seymour.[9] Perhaps he was not her type, or perhaps she believed that as a daughter of a leading peer and widow of the King's son, she could do better. Norfolk believed that in Mary's situation—she was penniless and not recognized as Henry VIII's daughter-in-law—she would have problems finding a new husband.[10] It has been recently suggested that Mary may have refused to marry Seymour because she feared that she would lose the title of Duchess of Richmond and the question of her jointure would never be settled.[11] Considering Mary's determination, this scenario is certainly plausible.

When the Seymour match backfired, the King decided to use Mary Howard, along with his other female relations, as pawns in the international marriage market. In October 1538, Henry VIII was eager to obtain the Duchy of Milan through the marriage of his elder daughter, Lady Mary Tudor, to Charles V's cousin, Dom Luis of Portugal. In order to secure the alliance, he was prepared to marry his younger daughter, Elizabeth, his niece, Margaret Douglas, and Mary Howard into the Italian nobility.[12] Mary was recognized as the King's former daughter-in-law and a member of the royal family, although yet again, nothing came out of this grand scheme and she was still penniless.

A letter written by Mary to Thomas Cromwell at an unknown date in 1538 suggests that she met Henry VIII in person during his recent summer progress and "submitted all my pretence of title unto his most gracious pleasure and order".[13] Mary's letter clearly shows that Cromwell used his influence to help her. The King, regularly pestered by Norfolk and Cromwell, eventually relented, and in March 1539, he finally made the first in a series of grants to Mary Howard.[14] By 1540, she had been granted a total income of £744 from various former Church properties. It seems that the King did not grant Mary her right out of pure kindness or sense of obligation, however. At some point in 1540, he fell in love with Mary's cousin, the teenaged Katherine Howard.

Despite the rumours that Henry VIII would marry Mary Shelton, the King decided to wed a German princess, Anne of Cleves. Anne set foot in England in December 1539, and Mary Howard, along with the King's niece Margaret Douglas, was included in the new Queen's reception. The new royal marriage survived only six months because Henry VIII was not impressed with his bride and claimed that he had "neither will nor courage" to consummate the match since he was appalled by "such displeasing airs as he felt with her". "The looseness of her breasts and other tokens" ensured the King that Anne of Cleves was not a virgin, and he decided to annul his marriage to her.[15]

Henry VIII desperately tried to wriggle free from his commitment because his affections were "alienated from the Lady Anne to that young girl Katherine". Katherine Howard was about sixteen when Henry VIII cast his appreciative eye on her. Her father, Edmund Howard, was the Duke of Norfolk's brother, and thus Katherine was Norfolk's niece and first cousin of Mary Howard and Anne Boleyn. Raised in the household of her step-grandmother, Agnes Howard, Dowager Duchess of Norfolk, Katherine developed into a young lady of attractive appearance and considerable music skill.

No one, apart from people who lived in Agnes Howard's household, knew that Katherine was not a virgin when she became the King's fifth wife. It remains a matter of debate among historians whether Katherine Howard became sexually active in her early teens because she wanted to or because she was abused by Henry Manox and Francis Dereham. When she appointed him as her secretary, Dereham started spreading suggestive rumours that he and Katherine Howard had been on intimate terms before she caught the King's eye. Dereham's outbursts quickly drew attention, but it was not until one of the young

Queen's former roommates stepped forward with damning revelations that the scale of Katherine Howard's activities came to light.

On 13 November 1541, the young Queen's household was broken up, and the ladies of her Privy Chamber, including Mary Howard and Margaret Douglas, were informed about "certain offences" that Katherine had done "in misusing her body" before her royal marriage took place.[16] The Queen was relocated to the Syon Abbey, where Margaret Douglas languished after her disgrace in 1536.

This time, just like four years earlier, Margaret found herself very close to incurring the King's wrath all over again. A letter from Ralph Sadler to Archbishop Cranmer dated 11 November 1541 indicates that Margaret Douglas had fallen in love with Katherine Howard's brother, Charles:

"His Majesty's pleasure is also, that tomorrow, after this declaration made, you shall call apart unto my Lady Margaret Douglas, and first declare unto her how indiscreetly she hath demeaned herself towards the King's Majesty; first, with the Lord Thomas and, secondly, with the Lord Charles Howard: in which part you shall by discretion, charge her with overmuch lightness and, finally, give her advice to beware the third time, and wholly apply herself to please the King's Majesty, and to follow and obey that shall be His Highness's will and commandment; with such other exhortations and good advices as by your wisdom you can devise to that purpose."[17]

Considering that Margaret was only warned to be careful the next time and chastised by Archbishop Cranmer, her affair with the Queen's brother must have been innocent in comparison to her earlier romantic attachment to Lord Thomas Howard. Nothing more is known about this affair. The couple probably split at some point in November 1541 because Margaret left court at that time, and Charles Howard was seen riding with his brother about the town in December "to show that they did not share the crimes" of their sister.[18] The Privy Council's instructions touched upon the matter of what to do with the Queen's female servants, including Margaret Douglas and her friend, Mary Howard:

". . . and my Lady Margaret Douglas to be conducted to Kenninghall, my Lord of Norfolk's house, in Norfolk; in whose company shall also go my Lady of Richmond, if my lord her father, and she, be so contented."[19]

It is from the safety of Kenninghall that Margaret Douglas and Mary Howard awaited the news from court. It has been suggested that Mary Shelton joined them there after Katherine Howard's downfall, but there is no evidence to that effect.[20]

On 7 December 1541, the French ambassador Marillac reported that the Duke of Norfolk, whose "influence is much diminished", left court.[21] It is from his luxurious residence at Kenninghall that Norfolk penned an obsequious letter to Henry VIII eight days later. Norfolk, who was "prostrate and most humble" at the feet of his sovereign, sought to distance himself from his "two false traitorous nieces", Anne Boleyn and Katherine Howard. They bore him "small love", he felt obliged to remind Henry VIII. Norfolk also tried to distance himself from his "ungracious stepmother", Agnes Howard, who raised the young Queen and turned a blind eye to her behaviour. Norfolk also condemned his "unhappy brother and his wife, with my lewd sister of Bridgewater", all of whom knew about Katherine Howard's secrets and were promptly committed to the Tower.[22]

Meanwhile, the evidence against the young Queen was mounting. During the course of the investigation, it came to light that Katherine Howard had attended a series of late-night meetings with a gentleman of Henry VIII's Privy Chamber, Thomas Culpeper. Although she could not have been executed for her pre-marital sexual experience, her clandestine meetings with Thomas Culpeper were an entirely different matter. Although the Queen claimed that it was her lady-in-waiting, Lady Jane Rochford, widow of George Boleyn, who procured and organised the meetings, and that Culpeper never knew her carnally, the King decided to punish those who played him for a fool. Dereham and Culpeper met their grisly ends at the scaffold on 10 December 1541. Katherine Howard and her lady-in-waiting, Lady Rochford, were executed two months later.

Mary Howard's brother witnessed their deaths. The Queen was "so weak that she could hardly speak", but she and Lady Rochford "made the most godly and Christian end that was ever heard tell of".[23] Many members of the Howard clan were found guilty of misprision of treason and sentenced to "perpetual imprisonment", although they were released in August 1542.[24] It is sometimes alleged, in fiction as well as in historical textbooks, that Mary Howard was committed to the Tower with her relatives. This is not the case, however. Those who were incarcerated were specifically charged with knowing about Katherine Howard's past but not mentioning it to Henry VIII. Mary could have had no knowledge about her cousin's activities within their step-grandmother's household, and she was not even interrogated in relation to her cousin's case.

On 12 July 1543, Henry VIII took Katherine Parr as his sixth and final wife before a small audience of family and friends in the privy oratory known as the Queen's Closet in Hampton Court Palace. Although Mary Howard was not present at the wedding (as her friend, Margaret Douglas was) she had a lot in common with the new Queen and soon discovered that Katherine wanted to become her friend.

Katherine Parr was thirty years old when she married Henry VIII, and she was already twice a widow. Unlike Katherine Howard, she was mature, self-composed and interested in the New Religion. Mary had been included in Katherine Parr's circle at court, serving as an "extraordinary" member of the Queen's Privy Chamber.[25] This meant that Mary did not serve the Queen on a daily basis but was summoned to court whenever a great occasion required her presence.[26] One such occasion of state was a visit by the French embassy in the summer of 1546, when Mary arrived at court and was reunited with her friend, Margaret Douglas, and was also able to interact with Henry VIII's daughters, the Ladies Mary and Elizabeth, who served as the Queen's "ordinary" ladies.[27]

When Mary was not at court, the Queen also remembered her; in September 1544, one of Katherine Parr's servants was paid for "carrying a stag from Woking to the Duchess of Richmond".[28] Lady Mary Tudor was equally generous when the yeoman of her cellar was given 8s "to my Lady of Richmond", presumably as a gift.[29]

It is certain that the Queen included Mary in her circle because of Mary's religious beliefs. Mary was becoming more and more open with her approval of the teachings of the New Religion and enjoyed debating the Bible with like-minded friends so much so that her elder brother, Surrey, warned her from "going too far in reading the Scripture".[30] Mary's younger brother, Thomas, shared her religious zeal and was censured by the Privy Council for his "indiscreet proceedings touching talking of the Scripture matters".[31] During the Easter season of 1545, Mary made her beliefs clear when it was reported that "my Lord of Suffolk, my Lord of Arundel and my Lady of Richmond" had broken the Lenten fast.[32]

Katherine Parr surrounded herself with reform-minded ladies-in-waiting who studied the Bible each Sunday in the Queen's private lodgings. Mary was not a regular servant of Katherine Parr's, and she managed to stay away from the dangerous religious persecution that broke over the court in the last years of Henry VIII's reign. Katherine Parr herself narrowly escaped imprisonment and the threat of execution in 1546 when the Catholic faction accused her of being too bold in her "heretical" beliefs. The Queen's religious views became too extreme for Henry VIII's tastes, and the Catholic faction played on his fears and suspicions.

In the end, however, Katherine found her way out of trouble when the warrant of her arrest miraculously found its way to her chambers a day before the actual arrest. Although she managed to convince Henry that in her womanly naivety she thought that religious disputes provided a harmless way of distracting Henry from his health problems, Katherine Parr never debated religion with him again and kept her religious literature under lock and key. The Reformers would have to wait until Henry VIII's death to feel safe.

NOTES

[1] *Letters and Papers*, Volume 12 Part 2, n. 1187.
[2] St Clare Byrne, *The Lisle Letters*, Volume 5, p. 10.
[3] Ibid.
[4] Norton, *The Boleyn Women*, p. 213.
[5] *Letters and Papers*, Volume 10, n. 908.
[6] St Clare Byrne, op.cit., p. 184.
[7] Head, *The Attainder of Lord Thomas Howard*, p.13.
[8] Maclean, *The Life of Sir Thomas Seymour*, p.4.

[9] *Letters and Papers*, Volume 21 Part 2, n. 555.

[10] Everett-Wood, *Letters of Royal and Illustrious Ladies*, Volume 2, p. 374.

[11] Murphy, *Bastard Prince*, p. 127.

[12] *Letters and Papers*, Volume 13 Part 2, n. 4.

[13] Everett-Wood, op.cit., Volume 2, p. 378.

[14] *Letters and Papers*, Volume 14 Part 1 n. 651.

[15] Hutchinson, *The Last Days of Henry VIII*, p. 29.

[16] *State Papers, King Henry the Eighth*, Volume 1, pp. 691-692.

[17] Everett-Wood, op.cit., Volume 2, p. 294.

[18] *Letters and Papers*, Volume 16, n. 1426.

[19] *State Papers, King Henry the Eighth*, Volume 1, pp. 691-692.

[20] Hart, *The Mistresses of Henry VIII*, p. 127.

[21] *Letters and Papers*, Volume 16, n. 1462.

[22] Strickland, *Lives of the Queens of England*, p. 321.

[23] Ibid., p. 326.

[24] Hutchinson, *House of Treason*, p. 150.

[25] *Letters and Papers*, Volume 21 Part 1, n. 969.

[26] Evans, *Ladies-in-Waiting*, p. 33.

[27] *Letters and Papers*, Volume 21 Part 1, n. 1384.

[28] *Letters and Papers*, Volume 19 Part 2, n. 688.

[29] Madden, *Privy Purse Expenses of the Princess Mary*, p. 171.

[30] Childs, *Henry VIII's Last Victim*, p. 264.

[31] *Letters and Papers*, Volume 21 Part 1, n. 769.

[32] Bridgen, *Henry Howard, Earl of Surrey and the 'Conjured League'*, p. 523.

CHAPTER 13:
MARRIAGES AND DEATHS

As the King's niece, Margaret Douglas was a valuable pawn in the international marriage market, but it seems that she extracted an unusual promise from Henry VIII concerning her future marriage. When Matthew Stuart, Earl of Lennox, sought to marry Margaret, the King replied that although he "could be contented" if the said marriage took effect, he "promised our niece never to cause her to marry any but whom she shall find in her own heart to love".[1] Therefore, the King believed it was necessary for Margaret and Matthew to meet first and see if they liked each other.

Luckily, Margaret liked what she saw and fell in love with Matthew. Their wedding was celebrated at St James's Palace on 29 June 1544, with Henry VIII and his wife in attendance. Margaret became the Countess of Lennox and was referred to as such in diplomatic dispatches. Her marriage to Matthew Stuart was a very happy union; her husband often referred to her as his "Good Meg" and relied on her advice. After her wedding, Margaret alternated between residing at her new family seat at Temple Newsam, a gift from Henry VIII, and her lodgings at court.

She was sometimes mentioned in the letters of other courtiers, such as the one written on 15 September 1544 by Richard Fane to Henry Knyvett: "I wish honour, long life and quiet minds unto my Lady Margaret's grace and my Lady Richmond, and no less to my Lord of Surrey."[2]

Despite the fact that Henry VIII kept his promise regarding her marriage, his relations with Margaret soured near the end of his reign, and he excluded his niece from the succession in his last will. Although it has been suggested by several historians that Margaret and her royal uncle had fallen out over religion, recent research conveyed by historian Leanda de Lisle proves that this is not the case. One of the King's trusted servants, Thomas Bishop, was also a former secretary of Margaret's husband. The Earl and Countess of Lennox complained to Henry VIII about Bishop, claiming that he was a troublemaker and a thief. The King, who valued Bishop's services, was angered by Margaret and Matthew's accusations so much so that Bishop recorded that Margaret lost the King's favour shortly before his death and never recovered it.[3]

Mary Shelton, who was once the King's mistress and one of the most popular girls at court, was still unmarried. At some point in the late 1530s, one of Mary's admirers— who, we do not know—betrayed her trust and boasted of their affair in public. Mary gave vent to her feelings in one of the poems copied into the *Devonshire Manuscript*, writing that she was unable to "make a joke of all my woe" and "cloak her grief". Paul G. Remley has suggested that Mary Shelton was "victimized by scandal and, apparently, wronged by one man in particular".[4]

It is tempting to link Mary's sudden departure from court with some sort of social scandal, especially in light of the knowledge gained from a list of pensions and grants to religious communities bestowed on 29 January 1539, showing Mary Shelton receiving a royal stipend of £4.[5] It is strange that merely a year after courtly gossip predicted she had a chance of becoming Henry VIII's next wife, Mary was sent away from court. Placing noblewomen in nunneries after scandals was a common practice among the Tudor elites; when Lady Anne Hastings's affair with the King was discovered in 1510, she was removed from court by her husband and taken sixty miles away to a convent.

Mary's entries in the *Devonshire Manuscript* clearly show that she was heartbroken because she described love as "the most stormy life". One particular line suggests that she was disillusioned with "some of the inequalities of her day, particularly in relation between the sexes". When transcribing a poem written by Chaucer, she altered many verses to give them a feminine slant. The original "cursedness yet and deceit of women", she exchanged for "the faithfulness yet and praise of women".[6] This strongly implies that she was not only wronged by her erstwhile admirer but also that she bemoaned the "double standard" of morality that regarded a sexual lapse by a woman as a badge of shame while male lapses were regarded as minor.

Mary did not stay in a convent for long. By the 1540s, she was in love with her first cousin, Thomas Clere. When Thomas died in 1545, the poet Surrey, Mary Howard's brother and Thomas Clere's close friend, included the telling line "Shelton for love, Surrey for lord thou chaste" in a verse epitaph composed for Thomas.

By 1546, Mary Shelton was married to Anthony Heveningham, a wealthy landowner who, like Thomas Clere, was her first cousin. Mary was Anthony's second wife and became stepmother to his children. It remains unclear how many children Mary and Anthony had together. The only source listing the offspring of Anthony Heveningham is his last will, where he mentions nine children in total, but we still do not know how many children he had by his first wife, Katherine Calthorpe, and how many children Mary bore him. We can, however, trace some of them in contemporaneous accounts and make our own conclusions.

Henry Heveningham, described in Anthony's will as his "son and heir apparent", was the eldest, and according to Francis Blomefield's *Essay Towards a Topographical History of the County of Norfolk,* he was born of Anthony's first wife.[7] Two other sons, Arthur and John, were presumably born by Mary, as Arthur Heveningham was described as the eldest son born to Mary and Anthony.[8]

When it comes to the six daughters of Anthony Heveningham listed in his testament—Mary, Ann, Jane, Abigail, Bridget and Elizabeth—only Abigail can be firmly established as Mary's daughter and traced through contemporaneous documents. She became a maid of honour to Queen Elizabeth in 1568, married Sir George Digby of Coleshill and continued her service in the Queen's Privy Chamber. A certain "Lady Digby" was listed among the Queen's servants in 1600; it could have been Abigail, but it has also been suggested that the woman in question may have been Lettice Digby, daughter of Gerald FitzGerald and wife of Sir Robert Digby.[9] If we are to assume that Anthony Heveningham listed his six daughters in order of their births—as he clearly did when mentioning his three sons—we may assume that they were all born by Mary Shelton, since the eldest, Mary, was named after her. It is through Arthur and Abigail that the Shelton-Heveningham bloodline continued well into the eighteenth century.

In 1546, Mary's name was again embroiled in a scandal. In December 1546, Mary's friend, the poet Surrey, fell out of favour with the King and was arrested on suspicion of treason. Mary was apparently close with Surrey, as the investigators were advised to "examine Mistress Heveningham, late Mary Shelton" in connection to a letter she received from him. Surrey had indeed instructed his servant to deliver a now lost letter that he had written to Mary: "I pray deliver this letter with all speed to Mrs. Heveningham, whom you shall find at Jerome Shelton's house in London, or else be there within three days". The letter must have been of utmost importance since Surrey added this injunction in a postscript: "Deliver this letter to none but her own hands".

Confronted with such evidence, the investigators judged that "it is thought that many secrets have passed between them before her marriage and since".[10] Unfortunately, Mary's deposition—and it is highly likely that there was one—did not survive to our times. It has been recently suggested that Mary and Surrey were lovers, "perhaps coming together in their mutual grief over Thomas Clere".[11] While this possibility may not be ruled out completely, the theory seems unlikely considering that Mary's husband, Anthony, displayed a great deal of affection and trust in Mary in his last will. It remains doubtful whether he would have done so if Mary had betrayed him with Surrey. It is worth remembering that Surrey was not only a brother of Mary's friend, Mary Howard, but also a member of the Devonshire group and the best friend of her former lover, Thomas Clere, so it was understandable that they remained on good terms.[12]

The fact that Surrey's letter was sent to Mary when she was staying at the London house of her cousin, Jerome Shelton, is telling and could shed a whole new light on the Shelton-Surrey relationship. Jerome Shelton was a money-lender, monastic estate manager, property speculator, bondsman and Exchequer official. Always in financial straits—"in the misery of debt", as he put it—Surrey was closely linked to the Shelton-Clere families, and the fact that Mary Shelton was "particularly close to Jerome" could and probably did help him to pay off some of Surrey's debts.[13] Unfortunately, the records of Jerome Shelton's money-lending activities do not survive, and this speculation must, for now, remain hypothetical.

Anthony Heveningham's last testament dates to 18 November 1557. He mentioned "Dame Marye

Heveningham, to have one-third of my manors and to be sole executrix". The fact that Anthony appointed Mary as his sole executrix is telling and provides a valuable hint that their marriage was a happy union founded upon mutual respect and trust. Anthony requested to be buried in the church of St Peter of Ketteringham, "according to the estate that God hath called me, remitting the order of my funeral to the consideration of my executrix, wishing the same quietly to take effect to the honour of God and the relief of the poor people."[14]

This is one of Mary Shelton's last appearances in the historical record; after that, she becomes merely a name on an ink-stained parchment. After Anthony's death on 22 November 1557, Mary married Philip Appleyard, who was listed among the witnesses of Anthony Heveningham's last will, and in 1567 they were described as "the Queen's servants", jointly receiving a crown lease of property at Whaplode, Lincolnshire.[15] The exact date of Mary's death is unknown, but her burial date is usually given as 8 January 1571.[16] The spot of her final burial also remains uncertain, but it is possible that she was buried with her first husband, Anthony Heveningham, at Ketteringham Church. In his last will, Anthony requested to be buried with Mary, and their intended tomb "on the north side of the chancel" was decorated with the arms of Heveningham and Shelton, although the inscription was lost during the course of history.[17] The Ketteringham Church still stands today as a silent reminder of Mary Shelton's life and death.

NOTES

[1] St Clare Byrne, *The Letters of King Henry VIII*, p. 347.

[2] *Letters and Papers,* Volume 18 Part 2, n. 190.

[3] De Lisle, *Tudor: A Family Story*, pp. 412-415

[4] Remley, *Mary Shelton and Her Tudor Literary Millieu*, p. 57.

[5] *Letters and Papers,* Volume 14 part 1, n. 1355.

[6] Remley, op.cit., p. 56.

[7] Blomefield, *An Essay Towards a Topographical History of the County of Norfolk*, Volume 1, p. 174.

[8] Ibid.

[9] *The Progresses and Public Processions of Queen Elizabeth: Volume IV: 1596 to 1603*, p.103.

[10] Remley, op.cit., p. 46.

[11] Norton, *The Boleyn Women*, p. 217.

[12] Clere and Surrey were very close friends, serving together in France during Henry VIII's last war campaign. Clere trusted Surrey so much so that when he believed himself to be close to death on the field, he handed Surrey his last will.

[13] Alsop, *The Financial Enterprises of Jerome Shelton*, p. 39., Childs, *Henry VIII's Last Victim*, p. 267.

[14] Harvey, *The Visitation of Norfolk in the Year 1563*, Volume 2, pp. 398-9.

[15] *Calendar of the Patent Rolls (1216-1566)*, p. 23.

[16] Heale, 'Shelton, Mary [married names Mary Heveningham, Lady Heveningham; Mary Appleyard] (1510x15–1570/71)', Oxford Dictionary of National Biography.

[17] Blomfield, *An Essay Towards a Topographical History of the County of Norfolk*, Volume 5, p. 94.

CHAPTER 14:
INTRIGUE AND CONSPIRACY

On 11 December 1546, hoofbeats disturbed the peace of a silent Tuesday morning. Three of Henry VIII's councillors—John Gate, Richard Southwell and Wymond Carew—came to Kenninghall Palace to interrogate Mary Howard and Bess Holland. The councillors found them "newly risen and not ready", although the two women "came to us without delay in the dining chamber". Upon hearing that her father and brother had been committed to the Tower for high treason, Mary was "sore perplexed, trembling and like to fall down". She was dismayed, but as soon as she collected herself, Mary let the King's servants know that she was prepared to cooperate with them:

". . . coming unto herself again, she was not, we assure Your Majesty, forgetful of her duty, and did most humbly and reverently upon her knees humble herself in all unto Your Highness, saying that although nature constrained her sore to love her father, whom she hath ever thought to be a true and faithful subject, and also to desire the well-doing of his son, her natural brother, whom she noteth to be a rash man, yet, for her part, she would nor will hide or conceal anything from Your Majesty's knowledge, especially if it be of weight, or otherwise, as it shall fall in her remembrance, which she hath promised, for the better declaration of her integrity to exhibit in writing unto Your Highness's most honourable council."[1]

The councillors then stated that they searched Mary Howard's coffers and chambers but "found no papers of consequence". Her chambers were, the report goes, "so bare, as Your Majesty will hardly think". Mary's jewels, as it turned out, had either been sold or pawned to "pay her debts as she, her maidens and the almoner do say". The Duke of Norfolk, as it became apparent, was not the most indulgent of fathers. He was, however, a very generous lover because Bess Holland's chambers were filled with expensive jewels and trinkets such as rings set with diamonds, golden brooches, strings of pearls, girdles, beads and buttons.

The Countess of Surrey, Mary's sister-in-law, was living at Kenninghall with her children and nursery women. The countess was heavily pregnant at the time, and the councillors observed that she was "looking her time to lie in at this Candlemas [2 February 1547]". To prevent distressing her any further, the Countess of Surrey was sent away. Mary Howard and Bess Holland were to depart for London the next day.

The reasons why Henry Howard, Earl of Surrey, was arrested and charged with high treason are unclear. The Duke of Norfolk was arrested by implication rather than for any offence he might have committed himself. Mary Howard observed that her brother was a "rash man", and the available evidence bears this statement out. Surrey was notoriously proud of his noble origin and detested "the new men at court", especially the Seymours. He was impulsive, hot-tempered and easily provoked to fight. Surrey was also preoccupied with wondering what would happen after Henry VIII's death, when nine-year-old Prince Edward would become king.

Henry VIII's deteriorating health—he was excessively corpulent, feverish and in constant pain emanating from his ulcerated legs—invited speculation about the regency that would follow his death. The members of the King's council jockeyed for position, and the Seymour brothers, Prince Edward's ambitious uncles, emerged as the strongest leaders of the new regime. Everyone at court new that those who allied themselves with the Seymours would become members of a very influential faction.

The Duke of Norfolk, politically savvy and always on the lookout for new opportunities, was well aware of this fact, and in 1546 he decided to offer Mary's hand in marriage to Thomas Seymour yet again. This time, however, Surrey was against the match because he believed that the noble Howards didn't need ambitious upstarts like the Seymours to advance themselves under Henry VIII's successor. Surrey believed he and his father deserved to have a place in the slowly forming protectorate; they would not scramble for power.

Mary, it seems, was not entirely hostile to the match, although she admitted that she was not inclined to marry Thomas Seymour.[2] The fact that Mary decided to consult her brother about the marriage may suggest that she, like her father, was aware that the Howards were in need of powerful allies. The piece of advice she received from Surrey horrified her and served as evidence during her brother's trial for treason. Surrey told Mary that "she should in no wise utterly make refusal" to Thomas Seymour, but feign indecision so that Henry VIII "should take occasion to speak with her again". With time, Surrey suggested, the King might "take such a fancy" to Mary that she might become his mistress and attain such influence as Francis I's sweetheart, the Duchess of Étampes, exerted in

France. Mary was not the kind of woman who would stoop so low. The thought of becoming Henry VIII's mistress appalled her, and she rebuked Surrey, telling him that "she would cut her own throat rather than she would consent to such a villainy".[3]

Surrey did two things that Henry VIII hated the most. First, he dared to speculate about the King's death, and Henry abhorred the thought of his own mortality. Second, Surrey insinuated that Henry VIII's royal person could be easily governed through his mistresses. Considering that the King's two executed wives were from the Howard clan, this insinuation held a sinister undertone. Although the King's health was rapidly deteriorating, he took a personal interest in Surrey's case. Poring through the documents and articles, feverish and aggravated by the pain in his legs, the King added corrections in his own hand. One of the articles concerned Mary:

"If a man [Surrey and, by implication, Norfolk] compassing with himself to govern the realm, do actually go about to rule the King and should, for that purpose, advise his daughter or sister [Mary Howard] to become his harlot, thinking thereby to bring it to pass, and so would rule both father and son [Henry VIII and Prince Edward], as by this next article does more appear, what it importeth [means]?"[4]

During his trial, Surrey was accused of exhorting Mary to use her body "to please the King and so to gain his favour". Surrey "emphatically denied the truth of the allegation" although, as the imperial ambassador reported, "he was shown a certain writing in the hand of his said sister in which she made this charge against him". Seeing the piece of paper, Surrey exclaimed: "Must I, then, be condemned on the word of a wretched woman?"[5] This situation mirrored the 1536 trial of Surrey's cousin, George Boleyn, who was shown a piece of paper with his wife's statement about the King's potency. George had allegedly exclaimed: "On the evidence of only one woman you are willing to believe this great evil of me and on the basis of her allegations you are deciding my judgement".[6] This may imply that statements given in court by women were sometimes regarded as malicious and, by implication, untrue.

Mary Howard's willingness to testify against her brother and father condemned her in the eyes of generations of historians. Some argued that Surrey, the great poet of his age, was incapable of giving his sister such vile advice, and she must have taken his sarcasm for its literal value. Historian Jessie Childs has pointed out that some historians and authors went as far as to "submit their own versions" of this particular episode.[7] Edwin Cassady, for instance, put imagined words into Surrey's mouth suggesting that Mary Howard was eager to marry Thomas Seymour, and that's why Surrey overreacted:

"You had best conclude your marriage quickly, while your husband-to-be is in such high favour. Then you can profit from your position to insinuate yourself into the good graces of the King. If you can submit yourself to such a husband, why not make the most of your chance?"[8]

This spirited monologue is fictitious and aims at condemning Mary for her willingness to marry Thomas Seymour. As has been noted earlier, Mary was not at all willing to contract marriage with Seymour, but she kept this option open and was prepared to discuss it with Surrey. Edmond Bapst, the nineteenth-century French biographer of Surrey, called Mary's deposition "a clever lie" and variously described her as a "vindictive sister" and a "hateful woman".[9] It is noteworthy that Mary's deposition was lost to the sands of time but not before it was seen by the seventeenth-century historian, Lord Herbert of Cherbury, who included its overview in his book, *The Life and Reign of King Henry VIII*. According to Cherbury:

" . . . the duke her father would have had her marry Sir Thomas Seymour, brother to the Earl of Hertford; which her brother also desired, wishing her also to endear herself so into the King's favour, as she might the better rule here as others had done; and that she refused . . ."[10]

The story of how Mary rebuked Surrey for his insinuation and how she exclaimed that she would rather cut her throat than become the King's mistress originally came from Sir Gawen Carew's deposition. Carew claimed that he knew about the altercation between Mary and Surrey from Mary herself. It is possible that Mary was confronted with Carew's statement and merely admitted that it was true. It seems almost impossible that a woman who was praised by her father for her outstanding intelligence would willingly confess something that could send her brother to the scaffold. His downfall would have been hers as well, and without her powerful male relatives to protect her, she would be all alone.

Surrey's apologists, including the anonymous author of the contemporary *Chronicle of King Henry VIII*, usually known as *The Spanish Chronicle*, tried to blacken Mary Howard's name to exonerate Surrey. *The Spanish Chronicle* claimed that it was Mary who stepped forward with the damning evidence, touching her brother's coat of arms, although other sources from Surrey's trial do not bear this statement out. In *The Spanish Chronicle*, it was Mary who denounced her brother's heraldic treason because Surrey dared to lecture her on her allegedly lax morals. If we are to believe this version of events, Mary Howard was flirtatious by nature, and Surrey was not happy about it:

"She was one of the most beautiful dames in the land, but she was young, and, it was suspected, too free with her favours."[11]

The chronicler goes on to say that Surrey and his brother, Thomas, "grieved at her mode of life" and Surrey chastised Mary, but she "took no notice of what the earl said to her, but gave herself up to her pleasures." Cleverly, the chronicler adds that before their relations went sour—that is, before upbraiding her—Surrey "always visited her, and showed great affection for her, telling her all his affairs". After upbraiding her, he prophesied:

"Sister, I am very sorry to hear what I do about you, and if it be true I will never speak to you again, but will be your mortal enemy."[12]

After putting these words in Surrey's mouth, the chronicler goes on to report the following story:

"And it appears that the earl had had a picture painted in which the arms of his father were joined to those of the King, and surrounded by the garter; and where the motto of the garter should have been 'Honi soit qui mal y pense', he put in English 'Till then thus', and then ordered the painter to put another painted canvas over it, so that it looked as if no other painting was there. The earl could not keep his secret from his sister, and he told it to the duke her father, who called the earl aside and rated him soundly about it, when the son replied, 'You know, Father, that our ancestors bore those arms, and I am much better than any of them, so do not grieve about it.' The duke said, 'My son, thou knowest that if it come to the ears of the King he may accuse thee of treason, and me too; so pray, keep it secret.' 'No one knows it, Father,' he said, 'but you and my sister, for the painter is Italian, and has gone to his own country.' This was the truth; and the duke said, 'God grant, my son, that no ill may come of it. Do not tell thy brother, Thomas, who is too young to be trusted, and might tell it to someone who might accuse us. Bring it to me, and let me see it'; to which the earl replied, 'Sir, it is impossible to see it, for another painting is over it.'

As the earl was offended with his sister, and had threatened her, and she on her part still continued her mode of life, without thinking of the great evil she was bringing on her father and brothers, she went to the King and said, 'Please, Your Majesty, my brother the Earl of Surrey, has had such-and-such a picture painted, I know not with what intention (and she described the picture to him), and as I have learnt it I thought well to tell Your Majesty, so that you may ask him his intention.'" [13]

What are we to make of this? Written in 1550 by an anonymous Spaniard living in London, *The Spanish Chronicle* is usually taken with a touch of reserve by historians because it provides sensationalised accounts littered with inaccurate names, dates and places. Mary's allegedly immoral conduct is not mentioned in other contemporaneous sources; quite the contrary, her father praised her for handling herself admirably after her husband's death.[14] Casting Mary Howard in the role of a pleasure-loving coquette, the anonymous chronicler gives her a good motive to act against Surrey and, surprisingly, he makes no mention about Surrey's suggestion that Mary should become the royal mistress. There is also no reference to the remaining charges against Surrey, other than usurping the royal coat of arms.

But how much truth is in the described scene? The chronicler apparently had some knowledge about the cause of Surrey's downfall because heraldic treason was among the most prominent crimes he was accused of. The Duke of Norfolk had indeed disapproved of his son's new coat of arms but, contrary to *The Spanish Chronicle*, he did not perceive it as treasonous. A painting in which Surrey was portrayed leaning against a broken pillar formed part of the charges, but the painting itself was not commissioned in strict secrecy, as *The Spanish Chronicle* implies; it was mentioned by several contemporaries. The painter was not Italian but the Dutchman William Scrots, who succeeded Hans Holbein as court painter. The portrait was inscribed with the Latin motto 'Sad superset' ("Enough survives") and not 'Till then thus'.

Also, Surrey never hid his coat of arms from anyone; he had his controversial quarterings painted into escutcheons "in the presence of the King's Highness's Council". He also displayed his arms "in full public view" at Kenninghall.[15] In fact, Surrey consulted the Garter King of Arms about his right to bear the "arms of Brotherton and St Edward and Anjou and Mowbray quartered, and said he would bear it" even when warned that "it was not his honour to do so". Surrey's servants later deposed that the arms of his bedhead much resembled those of the King.[16]

Thus *The Spanish Chronicle's* claims that only Mary Howard knew about her brother's painting and his controversial coat of arms are far removed from the truth. Also, she did not denounce her brother for his armorial bearings; according to an imperial ambassador, Surrey's arrest was triggered by "a letter of his, full of threats, written to a gentleman".[17]

According to Lord Hebert of Cherbury, Mary was careful in her statements and said nothing that could put her father in danger. As to remarks about her brother, Mary repeated some of his "passionate words . . . little to his advantage, yet they seemed much to clear her father". Surrey's hatred of the new nobility was well known; nothing Mary said was particularly damaging to Surrey's reputation or surprising to the investigators. As to his coat of arms, Mary was careful enough to state that "she thought" that Surrey had "seven rolls" of armorial bearings, but these were never found. In her deposition, she did not make accusations against Surrey's coat of arms but carefully treaded about the subject, revealing nothing that could be used as evidence against him.

Bess Holland, on the other hand, had no qualms about implicating both Surrey and Norfolk. "The Earl of Surrey loved her not", Norfolk's mistress confessed, adding that there was also no love lost between Mary and Surrey either. Bess said that "she had addicted herself much" to Mary; indeed, the two seemed to get along very well, to the Duchess of Norfolk's chagrin. Everything Bess said about Norfolk seemed to point out that he felt that other men, presumably the Seymours and their adherents, disliked him because he was an old nobleman with a conservative view of religion. The most damaging evidence given by Bess concerned Norfolk's opinions about the King himself. "The King was much grown of his body, and he could not go up and down the stairs, but was let up and down by a device"; Norfolk may well have confided something like this to his mistress, but it was treason to talk about the King in this way. Bess claimed that Norfolk told her that Henry VIII was "sickly and could not long endure"; this verged on treason because it was forbidden to predict the monarch's death.

Meanwhile, in the Tower, Norfolk was trying to figure out what exactly happened. He was intelligent enough to grasp that he and Surrey had fallen victim to a courtly coup and insisted on a private audience with the King so that he could explain everything and clear himself off the false charges levelled against him. Norfolk knew that he had been arrested because of Surrey's indiscretions, but he was far from being defeated. Penning defensive letters to the King, he tried to remind Henry VIII of his long years of service.

In the past, Norfolk had acknowledged his "foolish son's demeanour" and interceded on his behalf whenever Surrey found himself in need of a rescue. Now, when he finally realized that the King's wrath against them was too strong, he decided to acknowledge their alleged faults and throw himself on Henry VIII's mercy, but it was to no avail. Surrey was executed on 19 January 1547, while Norfolk was saved only by Henry VIII's own death.

NOTES

[1] Everett-Wood, *Letters of Royal and Illustrious Ladies,* Volume 3, p. 202.
[2] See the discussion of Mary's marriage prospects in Chapter 12.
[3] *Letters and Papers,* Volume 21 Part 2, n. 555.
[4] Hutchinson, *House of Treason,* p. 191.
[5] *Calendar of State Papers, Spain,* Volume 9, n. 16.
[6] Although Ives in *The Life and Death of Anne Boleyn* (p. 331) takes these words as a reference to Jane Boleyn, it is equally possible that George was referring to one of three other women who were named as his and his sister's accusers.
[7] Childs, *Henry VIII's Last Victim,* p. 261.
[8] Ibid.
[9] Bapst, *Deux Gentilshommes-Poetes de la Cour de Henry VIII,* pp. 354-356.
[10] Cherbury, *The Life and Reign of King Henry the Eighth,* p. 625.
[11] *The Chronicle of King Henry VIII,* p. 142.
[12] Ibid.
[13] Ibid., p. 143.
[14] As discussed in Chapter 10.
[15] Childs, op.cit., pp. 235, 285.
[16] Bridgen, *Henry Howard, Earl of Surrey and the 'Conjured League',* p.

528.

[17] *Calendar of State Papers, Spain,* Volume 8, n. 370.

CHAPTER 15:
THE WIND OF CHANGE

The political and religious landscape changed after Henry VIII's death. As soon as the old King died, his last will was bypassed, and instead of a regency council formed of men with equal status, one man was chosen as Lord Protector. This man was Edward Seymour, who was largely responsible for the fall of the Howard men.

With her brother executed and her father languishing in the Tower of London, Mary Howard found herself in a difficult situation. Henry Howard's execution and the Duke of Norfolk's imprisonment were followed by the confiscation of everything they owned, which was more than any person who lived in Tudor England, besides the King himself, could dream of. Rich clothes made of elaborate materials such as silk, cloth of gold and satin, jewellery and objects of daily use made in sumptuous fashion, were all packed and taken away. Edward Seymour, Duke of Somerset and now the all-powerful Lord Protector, received Norfolk's clothes "however much worn: his parliamentary robes, jewels, gold chains, the French order of St Michel and the Garter regalia; crosses, brooches, rings, bracelets" and "most of his chapel plate".[1] Lands and estates were parcelled out between the men who clustered around the nine-year-old King Edward VI. Even the Howard family seat at Kenninghall was no longer in Mary Howard's possession, as it became Lady Mary Tudor's principal East Anglian residence under Edward VI.

We do not know why, but after Henry Howard's execution, it was Mary who received wardship of his children. Considering the fact that she lived in Kenninghall with them for years, she was someone they knew well and, as later evidence points out, they respected and cherished her. The question that begs to be asked is why Henry Howard's widow, Frances, was not appointed as her own children's guardian. One of the explanations may be the fact that her husband's execution stunned her to the point of losing the ability to take care of her sons and daughters. Although Frances was condemned by some nineteenth-century historians for her quick recovery after Henry Howard's tragic death, his execution had a large impact on her life. What happened to the child she was expecting in December 1546 remains unknown. Considering that Henry VIII's councillors estimated that she would give birth at the end of February 1547, she must have been in her seventh month of pregnancy, and it is possible that the shock of her husband's execution caused her to give birth to a stillborn child.

In the early reign of Edward VI, Mary moved to Reigate Castle with her brother's children. At some stage, she appointed John Foxe, the future martyrologist and author of *Actes and Monuments,* as tutor to her wards in order to "instruct them both in manners and learning, in which charge he deceived not the expectations of the duchess, a woman of great wisdom, had of him".[2] The children conveyed to his care were Thomas, who succeeded to the dukedom of Norfolk; Henry, afterwards the Earl of Northampton; and Jane, who became Countess of Westmorland. Surrey also had two daughters, Margaret and Catherine, who lived with Mary but were not tutored by Foxe. In 1572, Mary's eldest nephew, Thomas, was executed for treason. In his execution speech, he confessed:

"I have not been popishly inclined ever since I had any taste for religion, but was always averse to the popish doctrine, and embraced the true religion of Jesus Christ, and put my whole trust in the blood of Christ, my blessed Redeemer and Saviour."

It was John Foxe and Mary Howard who gave Thomas Howard, the fourth Duke of Norfolk, his first taste of reformed religion, and he never forgot about it. Mary Howard's household became something of a safe haven for the followers of the New Religion and a centre of learning during the reign of Edward VI. Mary received several dedications from protestant authors, including one from Thomas Becon, who wrote:

"This little treatise, most virtuous lady, I send unto your grace, as a testimony of my ready bent good-will and serviceable heart toward your grace, being provoked hereunto through your exceeding love and fervent zeal, which your most honourable ladyship bear, both toward the word of God, and the true professors of the same; most humbly beseeching your grace to take in good part this my rude and simple gift."[3]

In a work dedicated to Philip Howard, Earl of Arundel—the only son of the fourth Duke of Norfolk—Mary Howard's household was mentioned:

"His father, Thomas, Duke of Norfolk, was a prince of a very moderate disposition and moral good life, though not a little tinctured with heresy, by reason of his education in his aunt's the Duchess of Richmond's house, which was a receptacle and harbour of pernicious persons tainted in that kind, and in particular of the infamous apostate, John

Bale [who returned from exile in 1547 straight into Mary's household], and also of John Foxe, the author of the pestilent book, the *Actes and Monuments*".[4]

This view, written by a hostile Catholic, is a testament to the strength of Mary Howard's religious beliefs. It is tempting to speculate that service within the household of Anne Boleyn shaped Mary Howard's early religious beliefs. Although Anne's personal faith is a matter of fierce debate among historians, it is certain that she was anti-papal, keen on reforming the Church from within and eager to promote reading the Bible in vernacular. Mary enjoyed reading the Scriptures and debating their contents, as we have seen earlier. After Edward VI's death, however, the religious climate in England changed. Accession of the Catholic Mary Tudor, Katherine of Aragon's daughter, marked the beginning of prosecution of the Protestants.

NOTES

[1] Hutchinson, *House of Treason*, p. 201.
[2] *The Actes and Monuments of John Foxe*, ed. Hobart Seymour, p.13.
[3] Becon, *The Catechism of Thomas Becon*, p. 556.
[4] Nichols, *Mary Richmond: Female Biographies of English History*, pp.480-87.

CHAPTER 16:
FADING INTO OBSCURITY

Thomas Howard, third Duke of Norfolk, remained imprisoned throughout the whole reign of Edward VI. Mary Howard never stopped hoping that she could secure her father's release, but she wisely waited for the right moment to intercede on his behalf with the privy councillors. Politically astute, Mary knew that as long as Edward Seymour governed the realm as Lord Protector, she had no chances of helping her father. Seymour's arrest in October 1549 opened up a new possibility, and Mary was quick to grasp it. On 15 December 1549, Richard Scudamore wrote to Philip Hoby, the resident ambassador at the imperial court, that:

"My Lady of Richmond hath gotten licence of the council that she might have access to her father, and to begin sat with him yesterday by the space of three long hours."[1]

We may only imagine what this reunion looked like after two years of not seeing each other. On 26 December 1549, Scudamore informed Hoby that Mary was "so diligently" pleading for her father's release that many old enemies of the duke were afraid she might actually succeed. Mary was so efficient that she managed to improve the conditions of Norfolk's imprisonment; "she had gotten her father's lodging to be hanged with tapestry, his windows glazed, and also certain plate appointed him to be served with".[2] The Privy Council agreed that Mary and her mother, Norfolk's estranged wife, could visit him "at times and with train convenient, the Lieutenant [of the Tower] being present". A decision was also made to allow Norfolk to "walk in the garden and gallery when the Lieutenant shall think good."[3]

With the accession of Mary Tudor, many followers of the New Religion, including John Foxe, fled from the country in fear of prosecution. Mary Howard stayed and received an unexpected gift from the new Queen. Without waiting for the formality of reversing Norfolk's attainder, Mary Tudor released the duke from the Tower on her arrival to London in August 1553. Among the prisoners kneeling on the green before the chapel of St Peter ad Vincula within the Tower precinct was Thomas Howard, now aged almost eighty and still under sentence of death since the last months of Henry VIII's reign. Raising the prisoners one after another, Queen Mary kissed them and granted them their liberty.

Norfolk was now restored to favour and participated in Mary Tudor's coronation; he even led one last military campaign in the Queen's name. But his health was failing, and he knew his death was approaching. In his last will, Norfolk acknowledged Mary Howard's efforts. A daughter whom he once deemed to have been "too wise for a woman" did everything in her power to save him from the cold, damp prison cell in the Tower:

"Unto my daughter the Lady Mary Duchess of Richmond the sum of £500, as well in consideration that she is my daughter, as that she hath been at great costs and charges in making suit for my delivery out of imprisonment, and in bringing up my said son of Surrey's children."[4]

In the end, Mary was the only woman and, indeed, the only person in Norfolk's life who had never failed him. Interestingly, the duke's last will makes no mention of his estranged wife (his former mistress, Bess Holland, died in 1548). Thomas Howard died on 25 August 1554, aged eighty-one and surrounded by his family members.

And what about Mary? It is possible that she willingly chose to retire from court. There could have been no warm feelings between her and Queen Mary, as Mary Howard was known for her support of the Protestant religion and used to serve as "one of the chief and principal" maids of Anne Boleyn.[5] Queen Mary always hated Anne, and even years after her execution, she could not bring herself to forgive her former stepmother for what she saw as the ruining of Katherine of Aragon's life. Hatred of Anne Boleyn overshadowed the Queen's relationship with Anne's only daughter, Elizabeth, and it is possible that Queen Mary deliberately sought to distance herself from anyone who supported the Boleyn queen. On the other hand, it is possible that Mary Howard's health started to deteriorate, and she chose to retire from court for this reason.

Members of her family, including her nephew Thomas, whom she raised, flew high in Queen Mary's good graces. After the old Duke of Norfolk died in 1554, Thomas Howard, his grandson, succeeded him as the fourth Duke of Norfolk. When Thomas's son, Philip—named after Queen Mary's husband, Philip of Spain—was christened in Whitehall Palace in 1557, the royal couple was present, as was Mary's mother, Elizabeth Stafford Howard, now bearing the title of Dowager Duchess of Norfolk.[6] Mary did not appear at the ceremony.

Mary Howard disappeared from the records soon after her father's death. Although the exact date of her death is in dispute, she certainly died before 18 December

1555 since William Cordell, esquire, was granted "parcels of the lands of Mary, late Duchess of Richmond" on that date.[7] Sadly, nothing is known about the cause of Mary's death. Considering the fact that she was relatively young, aged about thirty-six, her death might have been unexpected. As a widow, she was entitled to write her last will, but if she ever sat down to compose it, it did not survive. It is unfortunate that a woman who lived such an extraordinary life slipped away so quietly, leaving no clues as to the cause of her early death.

After the dissolution of Thetford priory, where her husband was buried among her ancestors, Mary Howard's resting place was designated to Framlingham Church in Suffolk. There is no doubt that Henry Fitzroy's remains were carried off from Thetford to Framlingham because Mary's father asked for permission to transfer the body of his father, together with "the body of the late Duke of Richmond, the King's natural son" and other members of the Howard clan, in his petition to Henry VIII in 1539.[8] The vaults beneath the tombs of Henry Fitzroy, Duke of Richmond, and Thomas Howard, third Duke of Norfolk, were opened in April 1841. The manuscript account of the Reverend J.W. Darby, the Framlingham Church Reader, who was present at the opening of the vaults, was analysed by

John Ashdown-Hill. In Henry Fitzroy's vault, "there was found a skeleton entire, the coffin of wood having fallen to pieces". According to Darby:

"The body appeared to have been wrapped in many folds of cered cloth, and the teeth in the upper and lower jaw bones (fourteen in number in each) were quite perfect, and as the duke was only seventeen years old when he died, this was without doubt his skull, and the body must have been moved with the tomb".[9]

On the left side of Fitzroy's skeleton, there was found another body "wrapped in sheet lead". After cutting through the folds of lead, "the skull of an older person presented itself", but the conclusion that it was an older person's skull was based only on "the state of the teeth". Darby continued:

"There was a large hole in the front of this skull, as if the head must have had some severe blow at some time or other. The hair was in a good state of preservation and was of a fair or sandy colour. The bones were not sufficiently examined to make sure whether they were those of a female."[10]

Because this skeleton was found next to Henry Fitzroy, Darby wondered if it belonged to Mary Howard[11] or

162

to her great-grandfather, John Howard, first Duke of Norfolk, who was slain during the Battle of Bosworth in 1485. The head trauma corresponds with an injury John Howard sustained in battle because, as Darby pointed out, an arrow pierced through his head. Therefore it is highly unlikely that the skeleton with a head injury belonged to Mary Howard. But if her great-grandfather rested next to her husband after transferring their remains from Thetford to Framlingham, were exactly was Mary buried?

In total, Darby described six sets of human remains, but his descriptions were incomplete. Historian John Ashdown-Hill believes that among these six interments discussed by Darby are those that Mary Howard's father moved from Thetford priory to Framlingham Church shortly before Thetford's dissolution in 1540, as well as Norfolk's own remains. In his petition, Norfolk mentioned the bodies of his father, the second Duke of Norfolk, his son-in-law, Fitzroy, and his first wife, Anne of York (Norfolk's second wife and Mary's mother, Elizabeth Stafford Howard, requested to be buried in the Howard family chapel at St Mary's Church, Lambeth). Unfortunately, it will remain a mystery as to whether any of the skeletons belonged to Mary Howard, unless an occasion for the reopening of these vaults presents itself again.

NOTES

[1] *The Letters of Richard Scudamore to Sir Philip Hoby,* September 1549-March 1555, p. 102.

[2] Ibid., pp. 103-4.

[3] *Acts of the Privy Council of England,* Volume 2, p. 400.

[4] Nichols, *Mary Richmond: Female Biographies of English History,* pp.480-87.

[5] Foxe, *Book of Martyrs: The Actes and Monuments of the Church,* Volume 2, p. 372.

[6] *The Lives of Philip Howard, Earl of Arundel,* ed. by Fitzalan-Howard p. 5.

[7] *Calendar of the Patent Rolls Preserved in the Public Record Office: Philip and Mary,* Volume 3, p. 187.

[8] Ashdown-Hill, *The Opening of the Tombs of the Dukes of Richmond and Norfolk,* p. 4.

[9] Ibid., p. 2.

[10] Ibid.

[11] Whom he had mistakenly believed had never married Fitzroy.

Chapter 17:
"A VERY WISE AND DISCREET MATRON"

Margaret Douglas, Countess of Lennox, is the only one of the three heroines of this book who lived through the reigns of all of Henry VIII's children. At the closure of Henry VIII's reign, she withdrew from court to her estates in Yorkshire, where she devoted herself to raising her children. Her first child, Henry Stuart, Lord Darnley, died on 28 November 1545 and was buried in St Dunstan's Church, Stepney. Just over a week later, Margaret gave birth to another son, named Henry in honour of her deceased eldest boy.

Margaret spent most of Edward VI's reign at her estates in the countryside. The reason for her retirement was religion; Margaret remained deeply Catholic, while advisors to the young King were Protestants who pursued religious reform. As a member of the royal family, Margaret appeared at court on occasions of state. On 4 November 1551, the Dowager Queen of Scotland, Mary of Guise, visited England on her way to France, and Margaret

Douglas, together with her friend Mary Howard and other illustrious noblewomen (including Lady Jane Grey), welcomed the Dowager Queen and "brought her through London to Westminster".[1] Entries in Edward VI's diary show that Margaret was among the most illustrious entertainers of Mary of Guise, sitting at the Scottish Queen's right hand during an elaborate banquet. Margaret was not only a member of the English royal family; Mary of Guise was the widow of Margaret's half brother, James V of Scotland.

After Edward VI's death in 1553, the Catholic Mary Tudor ascended the throne. This was good news for Margaret Douglas, who once lived in Mary's household, where the two girls bonded over their difficult childhood and became close friends. Queen Mary's relations with her half sister, Elizabeth Tudor, deteriorated and she began to give Margaret precedence over Elizabeth, treating her as though she were heir presumptive, even though the conditions of Henry VIII's last will excluded Margaret from the line of succession.

In November 1553, the imperial ambassador reported that Queen Mary believed that if she had no heirs, Margaret Douglas "would be the person best suited to succeed" her. The Queen feared that if her despised half sister—born and raised as a Protestant—ascended the throne, she "might alter religion".[2] Queen Mary lavished expensive gifts on Margaret and gave her a set of splendid apartments in the royal palaces, but in the end, the Queen reluctantly accepted Elizabeth as her successor. Margaret's last service to Queen Mary was attending her funeral as chief mourner.

Although Margaret Douglas served as a maid of honour to Queen Elizabeth's mother, she now subscribed to a view arguing that, by canon law, Elizabeth Tudor was illegitimate and thus unfit to rule. Although she took part in Elizabeth's coronation, Margaret soon started plotting against the new Queen. As a direct descendant of Henry VII, Margaret believed that she and her son had a valid claim to the English throne. Elizabeth was well aware of this fact and tried to revive Henry VIII's old claim raised in 1536 of Margaret's alleged illegitimacy.[3]

One of Margaret's greatest ambitions was to see her dear son, Henry Stuart, Lord Darnley, married to the young Queen of Scotland. Mary Stuart, Queen of Scots, was the third child of James V and his wife, Mary of Guise, and thus Margaret's niece. Born on 8 December 1542, she was the only surviving child of Margaret's half brother, James. In the eyes of many Catholics, including Margaret Douglas, the young Queen of Scotland was the rightful heir to the English throne.

Descended from the Tudor line, and a Catholic at that, Mary was a perfect contender to the throne, and Queen Elizabeth was well aware of it. As a wife to the French Dauphin Francis, Mary was a formidable rival. Henry II of France proclaimed his eldest son and daughter-in-law King and Queen of England, and in France the royal arms of England were quartered with those of Francis and Mary. When Henry II died in 1559, fifteen-year-old Francis became King of France, with Mary, aged sixteen, as his Queen consort. Unfortunately, Francis II died in 1560, and Mary returned to Scotland. Soon afterwards, Margaret Douglas started planning her son's marriage to the Scottish Queen.

Margaret's first move was to send her twenty-year-old son to Scotland with condolences. Darnley cut a striking figure; he was very tall, blond and had piercing blue eyes. Margaret Douglas made sure that her son received an education fit for a king and had instructed him on how to act in Mary's presence. The young Queen of Scots would later recall that Margaret urged her to marry Darnley and tried to win her approval by sending her expensive gifts and letters.[4] Margaret was sure that Mary would accept

Darnley's advances and started telling everyone at court that they would rule Scotland together and replace Queen Elizabeth in England.

As soon as Elizabeth learned about Margaret's utterances, she summoned her whole family to London. Margaret's husband, Matthew, was locked in the Tower while Margaret and her children were put under house arrest. By July 1563, they managed to appease Queen Elizabeth's wrath and were reportedly "much made of" at court. Lord Darnley, "their son and heir, is also a daily waiter and playeth very often at the lute before the Queen, wherein it should seem she taketh pleasure, as indeed he plays very well."[5] In September 1564, Queen Elizabeth gave Matthew Stuart permission to return to Scotland and reclaim his titles and lands there. Margaret and Darnley remained in England.

Elizabeth knew that her Scottish rival was looking for a husband, and she proposed a match between Mary, Queen of Scots, and Robert Dudley. Dudley was Elizabeth's favourite and, some whispered, her lover. In October 1564, she elevated Dudley to the earldom of Leicester, with Darnley carrying the sword of state during the ceremony. Elizabeth suspected that neither Mary of Scotland nor her ambassador, James Melville, took Robert Dudley's candidature seriously. She asked Melville what he thought of Dudley and pointed at Darnley, saying; "Yet you like better of yonder long lad", hinting that she had full knowledge of Margaret Douglas's plot. Melville used his quick wit and diplomatic skills to appease Elizabeth, saying that "no woman of spirit would make choice of such a man that was more like a woman than a man, for he was lusty, beardless and lady-faced". But Melville knew how important Darnley was and later admitted that Margaret Douglas was a "very wise and discreet matron".[6] When he returned home, Margaret gave Melville some expensive jewels to present to Mary, Queen of Scots.

Margaret somehow succeeded in convincing Queen Elizabeth to allow Darnley to join his father in Scotland for three months. On 17 February 1565, Darnley met Mary, Queen of Scots, and both fell in love with each other. Melville later reported that Mary said that Darnley was "the lustiest and best-proportioned long man that she had ever seen".[7] When the period of three months was over, Queen Elizabeth summoned Darnley to England, but he refused to comply. Sensing trouble, she now demanded that Darnley and his father return home immediately, but to no avail. The only person Queen Elizabeth could punish was Margaret Douglas, who was confined to her chamber and later transferred to the Tower of London. In July 1565, Mary, Queen of Scots, married Lord Darnley in her private chapel at Holyroodhouse. Several months later, Margaret's husband wrote her a letter, saying:

"My Meg, we have to give God most hearty thanks for that King our son continues in good health and liking, and the Queen great with child, God save them all, for the which we have great cause to rejoice more. Yet of my part, I must confess I want and find a lack of my chiefest comfort, which is you . . ."[8]

Unfortunately, the marriage that Margaret desired so much turned out to be a failure. The young spouses started drifting apart, and even the birth of Prince James on 19 June 1566 did not bring them together. Darnley's tempestuous nature and outbursts of incontrollable jealousy alienated him from his wife. The bloodthirsty Scottish barons, who involved Darnley in the murder of Mary's Italian secretary, Rizzio, started having doubts about his role in Scottish politics. On 10 February 1566, Darnley's Edinburgh residence at Kirk o' Field was razed in a huge explosion. Darnley's partially-clothed body was discovered in a nearby orchard soon afterwards, strangled to death by an unknown attacker. The man who was held responsible for this murder, James Hepburn, Earl of Bothwell, was acquitted in the courts. He kidnapped Mary, Queen of Scots, and married her, causing great scandal in Scotland and abroad. Some murmured that Mary was complicit in Darnley's murder, but the question of her guilt or innocence falls beyond the scope of this book.

Queen Elizabeth sent two of her trusted ladies to inform Margaret Douglas of her son's murder. Margaret's grief over her beloved son's death was aggravated when she was told that her husband Matthew had also been killed. Margaret was so distressed at the news that the royal physician was summoned to restore her to health. It later turned out, however, that Matthew Stuart was still alive. Margaret's state of health was so fragile that Queen Elizabeth's secretary William Cecil, Lord Burghley, wrote:

"I hope that Her Majesty will have some favourable compassion of the said lady, whom any human nature must needs pity."[9]

Margaret was soon transferred from the Tower to house arrest at Sheen. When she was acquainted with all the particulars regarding her son's murder, she formed an opinion that Mary, Queen of Scots, was to blame. On 19 April 1567, Margaret and her husband were reunited, and together they wept bitterly over Darnley's death, as reported by Nicholas Throckmorton, who saw them.

Although it seemed that they would never have justice, in 1568 the Queen of Scots was defeated at the Battle of Langside and was forced to seek refuge in England. When Margaret and Matthew learned about this, they went to Queen Elizabeth, threw themselves on their knees before her and begged her to punish Mary. They wore "the deepest mourning", and Margaret's face was "all swelled and stained with tears". Margaret "cried so passionately for vengeance" that Queen Elizabeth lost her patience and sent the couple away, saying that "such accusations must not rest against the good name of a princess without further proof."[10] Elizabeth implied that none could slander an anointed queen's name with such grave accusations without solid proof of her involvement in Darnley's murder.

NOTES

[1] Burnet, *The History of the Reformation of the Church of England,* Volume 4, p. 222.

[2] *Calendar of State Papers, Spain,* Volume 11, n. 27.

[3] The annulment of her parents' marriage left Margaret's legitimacy intact. The attainder of Lord Thomas Howard in 1536 nevertheless referred on several occasions to Margaret as being her mother's "natural [illegitimate] daughter". This was Henry VIII's attempt to demote his niece in the succession and ensure the King's children had the superior claim. Read more about the attainder in Chapter 9.

[4] Marshall, *Queen Mary's Women,* p. 113.

[5] *Calendar of State Papers Foreign,* Elizabeth I, Volume 6, n. 1027.

[6] Marshall, op.cit., p. 115.

[7] Ibid., p. 116.

[8] Ibid., p. 117.

[9] Strickland, *Lives of the Queens of Scotland and English Princesses,* Volume 2, p. 412.

[10] Ibid., p. 418.

Chapter 18: "Not for Matters of Treason, but for Love Matters"

When James VI's regent was murdered in 1570, Margaret Douglas wanted her husband to succeed him, and Queen Elizabeth agreed. Many letters passed between Margaret and her husband, Matthew, while he was in Scotland; Matthew often wrote about their darling grandson, King James, who was the living memory of their murdered son, Darnley. Unfortunately, Matthew was assassinated on 4 September 1571, shot in the back during a skirmish with supporters of Mary, Queen of Scots, at Stirling Castle. His last thoughts were with James VI and his beloved Margaret. "If the babe is well, all is well", he said on his deathbed. He also spoke to the Scottish nobility, touchingly desiring them to "remember my love to my wife, Margaret, whom I beseech God to comfort".[1] Matthew Stuart, Earl of Lennox, was buried in the chapel at Stirling Castle, and news of his death reached England four days later. In a letter to Thomas Smith, Clerk of the Council, Lord Burghley sent the following instructions:

"Let Mr Sadler know hereof [about Matthew's murder]; but otherwise disperse [divulge] it not, lest it be not true that he is dead; and I would have no knowledge come to Lady Lennox before she shall have it from the Queen's Majesty."[2]

How Margaret took the news of her husband's murder remains unknown, but she probably reacted similarly as when she received the untrue tidings of his death several years earlier. After twenty-seven years of marriage, Margaret was a widow with only one surviving son. Of all her eight children, only Henry and Charles survived to adulthood. Now, with Darnley gone and Matthew murdered, Charles became the focus of Margaret's attention.

Darnley predeceased his father, and so the earldom of Lennox was granted to Charles by the Earl of Mar, who acted as the Regent of Scotland after Matthew Stuart's assassination. This grant was repealed when a new regent ruled that the Lennox title and all that went with it now belonged to Darnley's son, the Scottish boy King, James VI. Margaret and her son were left without revenues, although

Charles was known in England as the fifth Earl of Lennox. At nineteen, Charles was still unmarried, and Margaret started looking for a suitable bride for him. Her choice fell upon the Countess of Shrewsbury's daughter, Elizabeth Cavendish.

The Countess of Shrewsbury, better known as Bess of Hardwick, was a very wealthy and influential figure. Although Bess's daughter was beneath Margaret's son socially, the match was advantageous for both families. Bess's daughter would marry into royalty, and Margaret's son would never have to worry about money. Plus, the young people really liked each other. The two cunning mothers secretly negotiated the terms of marriage "for the best part of a year", and neither of them consulted Queen Elizabeth, who had the last say when it came to marriages among the nobility.[3] Recent events at court had clearly shown that the Queen was merciless when her role as a royal matchmaker was disregarded. Margaret and Bess, however, decided to shape their children's destinies by themselves, risking imprisonment and the Queen's wrath.

Bess invited Margaret and Charles to visit her and stay at the family property at Rufford Abbey. Upon their arrival, Margaret suddenly fell ill, and Bess took on the role of nurse, caring for her old friend while their children spent long days getting to know each other better. Charles fell in love with Bess's daughter Elizabeth, and the couple married within days in the chapel at Rufford Abbey.

When Queen Elizabeth found out about the marriage, she was furious. This match was of utmost importance since Charles Stuart was a direct male descendant of Henry VII, and any child born of his union to Elizabeth Cavendish could become yet another claimant to Elizabeth's throne.

The matter was further complicated by the fact that Bess of Hardwick and her husband were custodians of the captive Mary, Queen of Scots. Queen Elizabeth had already suspected that a friendly relationship was developing between Margaret Douglas and her former daughter-in-law, and she explicitly forbade Margaret to visit where the Scottish queen was kept. Margaret retorted that she could never forget about her son's murder, but there is evidence that she had already changed her mind as to who should be blamed for it. After Margaret's death in 1578, Mary, Queen of Scots, wrote:

"This good lady was, thanks to God, in very good correspondence with me these five or six years bygone, and has confessed to by sundry letters under her own hand, which I carefully preserve, the injury she did me by the unjust pursuits which she allowed to go out against me in her name through bad information, but principally, she said, through the express orders of the Queen of England and the persuasion of her council; who also took much solicitude that she and I might never come to good understanding together. But how soon (as soon as) she came to know of my innocence, she desisted from any further pursuit against me; nay, went so far as to refuse her consent to anything they should act against me in her name."[4]

From Mary's reminiscence, we may infer that Margaret forgave her in 1572 or 1573. Indeed, the two started exchanging correspondence and gifts. Elizabeth's fears of Margaret's meeting with Mary were thus well grounded, but the secret marriage between Charles Stuart and Elizabeth Cavendish took her by surprise. Some historians suspected that Margaret Douglas's illness at Rufford Abbey was feigned as it provided a convenient excuse for Margaret, who claimed that "other dealing or longer practice there was none, but the sudden affection of my son".[5]

When Margaret was summoned to court in December 1574, the French ambassador observed that she feared Queen Elizabeth would send her to the Tower. Indeed, Margaret was arrested while her son and his bride were confined to their house in Hackney. Upon hearing of her arrest, Margaret said: "Thrice have I been cast into prison, not for matters of treason, but for love matters."[6]

Queen Elizabeth refused to believe in Margaret Douglas's version of events because Bess of Hardwick's husband, the Earl of Shrewsbury, claimed the opposite in his letters. Charles Stuart, Shrewsbury said, was so "sick with love" that he "swore he would have no other wife but Elizabeth Cavendish". But while Margaret maintained that "the sudden affection" of her son was the reason behind his marriage to Elizabeth, the Earl of Shrewsbury claimed that the marriage was not as hasty or secretive as it seemed at first glance. According to Shrewsbury, this match "had been a talk between them [Margaret and Bess] more than a year past, not worthy of Her Majesty's hearing."[7] When Shrewsbury learned about Margaret's arrest, he felt obliged to write yet another long letter, saying that Margaret "was a subject in all respects worthy of Her Majesty's favour, and for the duty I bear to Her Majesty I am bound, methinks, to commend her as I find her. Yea, and to entreat you, and all my Lords of the Council, for her, to save her from blemish".[8]

Bess of Hardwick was never confined to the Tower and, having as many friends at court as she had, the Queen's anger soon melted away. Margaret Douglas was released from the Tower in March 1575, but she and the newlyweds were confined to the Lennox estates at Hackney throughout the summer.[9]

The marriage Margaret Douglas and Bess of Hardwick planned for so long bore its fruit in November 1575, when the baby girl Arbella Stuart was born. Although she was not a male heir, she was nevertheless welcomed, and the two proud grandmothers lavished gifts and attention on their sweet granddaughter. The sense of shared pride Margaret Douglas felt when Arbella was born is expressed in a letter addressed to Mary, Queen of Scots. Margaret thanked Mary "for your good remembrance and bounty to our little daughter".[10] Sadly, Arbella's father, Charles, died in March 1576, after a mere eighteen months of marriage to his beloved Elizabeth Cavendish. He was the last living child of Margaret Douglas, and now only Arbella and the young James VI of Scotland were Margaret's living legacies and the vehicles of her own ambition.

Arbella's relatives in England, including Margaret, believed that she was now the Countess of Lennox, a title she inherited from her father, but the Scottish government claimed otherwise and moved to repossess the Lennox lands in Scotland. Nevertheless, Margaret commissioned a portrait of Arbella, aged twenty-three months, defiantly labelling it as "Arbella, Countess of Lennox". In this portrait, Arbella is dressed in the finest gown with embroidered sleeves and a bejewelled headdress, clutching a doll dressed in the Spanish fashion. Around her neck hangs a shield with the countess's coronet and the Lennox motto expressed in French: "To achieve, I endure". Securing the Lennox title and lands would become one of Margaret Douglas's goals but, unfortunately, it would not be Margaret who would fight for them in Arbella's name.

NOTES

[1] Strickland, *Lives of the Queens of Scotland and English Princesses,* Volume 2, p. 427.
[2] Ibid., p. 428.
[3] Lovell, *Bess of Hardwick,* p. 245.
[4] Meline, *Mary, Queen of Scots and Her Latest English Historian,* p. 281.
[5] Strickland, op.cit., p. 438.
[6] Ibid., p. 439.
[7] Lovell, op.cit., p. 245.
[8] Ibid., p. 248.
[9] Ibid., p. 251.
[10] Steen, *The Letters of Lady Arbella Stuart,* p. 14.

CHAPTER 19:
"A LADY OF MOST PIOUS CHARACTER"

On 26 February 1578, Margaret Douglas sat down to compose her last will. The sixty-three-year-old Dowager Countess of Lennox, despite the royal blood running in her veins, was not a wealthy woman. The only valuables worth mentioning was the collection of twenty-one pieces of jewellery which she bequeathed to her precious little granddaughter, Arbella. They included such curious pieces as "a clock set in crystal with a wolf of gold upon it"; "a cross set with fair table diamonds, with a square linked chain"; "a rose set with fair diamonds"; "a carcanet set with table diamonds"; "a fair pearl chain" and others.[1]

Arbella Stuart was to inherit the jewellery if she reached her fourteenth birthday; if she died before that, then King James VI of Scotland was to receive them. Until that time, the precious Lennox jewels were to be kept in the custody of Thomas Fowler, the executor of Margaret Douglas's last will. Unfortunately, the jewellery intended for Arbella became the centre of controversy. Shortly after

Margaret's death, Fowler was robbed—or claimed to have been robbed—on a journey in Scotland. Somehow, the Lennox jewels found their way into the collection of King James VI of Scotland, Margaret's other grandchild.

Margaret Douglas, Dowager Countess of Lennox, died on 10 March 1578 amid speculations of poisoning. Although she was elderly and her health had already started to fail, her death occurred suddenly, and many people were shocked. Shortly before she fell ill, Margaret dined with Robert Dudley, Earl of Leicester, Queen Elizabeth's favourite and a man she used to scorn as a "pox-ridden wife murderer".[2] But by 1578, Margaret and Dudley had become allies, and in her last will, she left him a chain of pomander beads netted with gold and a tablet with a picture of Henry VIII.

Six years later, a scurrilous pamphlet known as *Leicester's Commonwealth* attacked Robert Dudley for his influence on Queen Elizabeth. Rumours that he had been the Queen's secret lover had been circulating at court and abroad from the early years of Elizabeth's reign, but *Leicester's Commonwealth* was so shocking in its accusations against Dudley that Francis Walsingham called it "the most malicious thing that was ever penned since the beginning of the world".[3] Although the accusations against

Dudley centred on his sexuality and alleged murder of his first wife, Amy Robsart, *Leicester's Commonwealth* also accused him of poisoning Margaret Douglas. This publication, written for propagandistic reasons, is the only contemporary source attributing Margaret's sudden death to poison. Considering that many accusations against Dudley in *Leicester's Commonwealth* were either outright lies or unfounded allegations, we should look upon the bit about Margaret Douglas's poisoning with a touch of reserve.

Margaret Douglas died in great debt, and the goods she possessed, even if sold, were not enough to cover the expenses of her funeral. Queen Elizabeth could not allow her first cousin to be buried like a pauper and so "of natural favour, pity and honour to her cousin", she covered the funeral expenses and paid off her debts out of the confiscated Lennox estates.[4]

The magnificent tomb in Westminster Abbey where Margaret lies buried was completed in October 1578 at the charge of Thomas Fowler, the executor of Margaret's last will. The tomb is decorated with kneeling figures of Margaret's eight children, four sons and four daughters, who all predeceased her. The Latin inscription on the tomb celebrates Margaret as "a lady of most pious character, invincible spirit, and matchless steadfastness", who was "mighty in virtue, mightier yet in lineage". Indeed, both of Margaret's grandchildren, Arbella Stuart and James VI of Scotland, were considered to be Queen Elizabeth's heirs. In the end, it was James VI who succeeded Elizabeth as James I of England. Margaret Douglas became "a progenitor of princes", as the inscription on her tomb proclaimed.

To Margaret Douglas, her grandson, James, was her "sweet and peerless jewel in Scotland", to whom she regularly sent valuable gifts.[5] Among the presents sent to James was a hawking glove set with rubies and pearls and several rings, including one with a pointed diamond.[6] Margaret Douglas was fond of fine jewellery, and one curious piece variously called "The Lennox Jewel" or "Darnley Locket" is still preserved in the Royal Collection. This heart-shaped golden locket with polychrome enamels was purchased in 1842 by Queen Victoria from Horace Walpole's collection. It remains unknown who commissioned the jewel or for whom it was intended. The description of the Lennox Jewel in the Royal Collection says:

"The Lennox or Darnley Locket is one of the most important early jewels in the Royal Collection. It is said to have been commissioned by Lady Margaret Douglas, Countess of Lennox (1515-78), for her husband Matthew Stuart, Earl of Lennox and Regent of Scotland, who fell in battle in 1571. Theories vary for which occasion the jewel was made. Generally, it is believed to have been a memorial piece following the earl's death and certainly before Margaret's own death, although the jewel makes no allusion to the earl's death. It has also been suggested that it was made to commemorate the return of the exiled earl to Scotland in 1564 or the restoration of his lands and honours in 1565."[7]

There are symbols referring to the house of Douglas and the Lennox coat of arms, as well as the monogram MSL—for Matthew and Margaret Stuart Lennox—surmounted by a wreath. Around the jewel's border runs the following verse: "Who hopes still constantly with patience shall obtain victory in their pretence". Above the heart the classical figures of Victory and Truth hold a crown set with three rubies and a table-cut emerald. The crown is surmounted by a fleur-de-lis upon an azure shield. It opens to reveal two hearts pierced by two arrows and the motto in sixteenth-century Scots: "What we resolve". The winged heart opens to reveal the device of two clasped hands and a green hunting horn surrounded by the inscription, also in Scots: "Death shall dissolve". Below this device is a skull and crossbones. The symbolism, initials and mottoes suggest that this piece of jewellery, intended to be worn around the neck or pinned on the breast, was certainly commissioned for or by Margaret Douglas.

It has been proposed that the jewel was given to Margaret in 1544 as a wedding gift from her first cousin, Lady Mary Tudor; it seems almost impossible since Lady Mary had no reason to use the lowland Scots in a motto. There are also historians, such as John Guy, who believe that the Lennox Jewel was commissioned by Margaret Douglas in 1565 and sent to Mary, Queen of Scots, as a wedding gift. It is known that Margaret gave Mary "a marvellous fair and rich jewel", and it was reported that everyone who saw it marvelled at its intricate craftsmanship; there was also a coded message for the Scottish queen.[8] Although there is no way of knowing whether this was the Lennox Jewel, it is highly likely.

The precious jewels Margaret Douglas bequeathed to her granddaughter, Arbella Stuart, became a matter of dispute in the 1590s. Arbella lost her mother in 1582 and became the ward of her maternal grandmother, Bess of Hardwick. When Bess learned that the jewels Margaret Douglas left Arbella mysteriously found their way to James VI's collection, she started petitioning the influential men at court for their return. Arbella turned fourteen in 1589, and by the terms of Margaret's testament, she should have already received the jewels. Bess of Hardwick petitioned Lord Burghley, and he made efforts to obtain the jewels. In June 1590, the English ambassador in Scotland reported to Lord Burghley:

"Sundry times I have moved the King, that the jewels late in the hands of Thomas Fowler, deceased, and appertaining to the Lady Arbella, might be restored to her. Nevertheless, I am still deferred, that upon sight of the Lady Margaret's will, the King will take order in all these things."[9]

In the end, the Scottish King told the English ambassador that he detained the Lennox jewels and other possessions of Thomas Fowler "in recompense of such legacies as the Lady Margaret Douglas bequeathed to him, and left in Mr Fowler's custody to be delivered to him". James also added that "these jewels and pearls" were treated as Thomas Fowler's personal belongings and, because Fowler died intestate, they now appertained to James himself.[10] It remains unknown whether James VI, who became James I of England upon Queen Elizabeth's death in 1603, ever returned Margaret Douglas's jewels to Arbella Stuart.

It is almost unbelievable how the fortunes of the descendants and relatives of Margaret Douglas, Mary

Howard and Mary Shelton were closely linked together. Mary Howard's nephew, Thomas, who inherited the dukedom of Norfolk in 1554, and who was raised by his aunt, was executed in 1572 for planning to marry Mary, Queen of Scots. When Charles I, James's son, was executed in 1649, the name of William Heveningham was amongst the regicides. William was the grandson of Arthur Heveningham, Mary Shelton's eldest son by her first husband, Anthony Heveningham. It is thus one of the unexpected twists of fate that Mary Shelton's great-grandson was one of the men responsible for the judicial murder of Margaret Douglas's great-grandson.

Despite the fact that Margaret Douglas, Mary Howard and Mary Shelton left their legacies, today they remain only footnotes in history. Although their contribution to posterity is enormous—the *Devonshire Manuscript* with their original and transcribed verses is still extant—they are overshadowed by other Tudor women, such as Henry VIII's six wives. Several letters of Margaret Douglas and Mary Howard survive, and their voices can be heard loud and clear across the centuries. Mary Shelton's poetry and her personal feelings recorded in the *Devonshire Manuscript* reveal a highly intelligent and talented woman.

Margaret Douglas, Mary Howard and Mary Shelton were energetic female courtiers who rose to prominence at the courts of successive Tudor monarchs and managed to survive and navigate through a multitude of courtly intrigues, although there is not one of them who did not lose loved ones in the process. The stories of these three forgotten Tudor women are truly remarkable and deserving of remembrance.

NOTES

[1] Cooper, *The Life and Letters of Lady Arabella Stuart,* p. 49.
[2] De Lisle, *Margaret Douglas at the Tudor Courts, History Today,* Volume: 63 Issue: 8 2013.
[3] Whitelock, *Elizabeth's Bedfellows,* p. 212.
[4] Cooper, op.cit., p. 53.
[5] Meline, *Mary, Queen of Scots and Her Latest English Historian,* p. 281.
[6] Strickland, *Lives of the Queens of Scotland and English Princesses Connected with the Regal Succession of Great Brittain,* Volume 2, p. 445.
[7] http://www.royalcollection.org.uk/collection/28181/the-darnley-jewel-or-lennox-jewel
[8] Guy, *My Heart is My Own,* p. 199.
[9] Cooper, op.cit., pp. 100-02.
[10] Ibid.

BIBLIOGRAPHY

A

Alsop, J.D. "The Financial Enterprises of Jerome Shelton, a mid-Tudor London Adventurer". *Guildhall Studies in London History,* vol. 4, no. 1. October 1979.

Ashdown-Hill, J. "The Opening of the Tombs of the Dukes of Richmond and Norfolk, Framlingham, April 1841: Darby's Account". *Ricardian 18 2008, 100-107* (later republished in *The Framlingham Journal*).

B

Bapst, E. *Deux Gentilshommes-Poetes de La Cour de Henry VIII.* Paris, 1891.

Baron, H. "Mary (Howard) Fitzroy's Hand in the Devonshire Manuscript". *Review of English Studies*, new ser. 45. 1994.

Betteridge, T., Lipscomb, S. *Henry VIII and the Tudor Court: Art, Politics and Performance.* Ashgate Publishing, Ltd., 2013.

Blomefield, F., Parkin, C., *An Essay Towards a Topographical History of the County of Norfolk, Volume III.*

Brigden, S. "Henry Howard, Earl of Surrey, and the 'Conjured League'". *The Historical Journal*, Vol. 37, No. 3. Sep. 1994.*The Letters of Richard Scudamore to Sir Phillip Hoby, September 1549-March 1555*. (ed.) Camden Miscellany 30. London, 1990.

C

Calendar of State Papers, Spain. Ed. Brewer, J.S. & Gairdner, J. Institute of Historical Research (1862-1932).

Cherbury, E. *The Life and Reign of King Henry the Eighth*. Mary Clark, 1683.

Childs, J. *Henry VIII's Last Victim: The Life and Times of Henry Howard, Earl of Surrey*. Thomas Dunne Books, 2007.

Clifford, H. *The Life of Jane Dormer, Duchess of Feria*. Burns & Oates, 1887.

Constantine, G. "A Memorial from George Constantine". Ed. T. Amyot, in *Archaeologia*, 23. 1831.

Cooper, E., *The Life and Letters of Lady Arabella Stuart: Including Numerous Original and Unpublished Documents, Volume 1*. Hurst and Blackett, 1866.

D

De Lisle, L., *Tudor: A Family Story*. Vintage Digital, 2013. Kindle edition.

"Margaret Douglas at the Tudor Courts". *History Today,* Volume: 63 Issue: 8. 2013.

E

Ellis, H., *Original Letters Illustrative of English History, Volume 2.* (2nd series). Harding and Lepard, 1827.

Evans, V.S., *Ladies-in-Waiting: Women Who Served at the Tudor Court*. CreateSpace Independent Publishing Platform, 2014.

Everett Wood, A. *Letters of Royal and Illustrious Ladies of Great Britain*. Three Volumes. H. Colburn, London. 1846.

F

Foxe, J. *The Actes and Monuments of the Church.* Ed. Hobart Seymour, M. Robert Carter & Brothers, 1855.

Fraser, W. *The Douglas Book. Four Volumes.* Edinburgh, 1885.

Friedmann, P. *Anne Boleyn: A Chapter of English History, 1527-1536*. Two Volumes. Macmillan and Co., 1884.

G

Guy, J. *My Heart is My Own: The Life of Mary, Queen of Scots.* Fourth estate, 2004.

H

Hall, E. *Hall's Chronicle.* J. Johnson, 1809.

Harris, B. *English Aristocratic Women, 1450-1550: Marriage and Family, Property and Careers.* Oxford University Press, 2002.

"Marriage Sixteenth-Century Style: Elizabeth Stafford and the Third Duke of Norfolk". *Journal of Social History*, Vol. 15, No. 3, Special Issue on the History of Love. Spring 1982.

Hart, K. *The Mistresses of Henry VIII.* The History Press, 2009.

Harvey, W. *The Visitation of Norfolk in the Year 1563, Volume 2.* Agas H. Goose, 1895.

Hayward, M. *Dress at the Court of King Henry VIII.* Maney Publishing, 2013.

Head, M.D. "Beyng Ledde and Seduced by the Devyll: The Attainder of Lord Thomas Howard and the Tudor Law of Treason". *The Sixteenth-Century Journal*, Vol. 13, No. 4. Winter, 1982.

The Ebbs and Flows of Fortune: The Life of Thomas Howard, Third Duke of Norfolk. University of Georgia Press, 1995.

Heale, E. "Shelton, Mary (1510x15–1570/71)". *Oxford Dictionary of National Biography.*

"Women and the Courtly Love Lyric: The Devonshire MS (BL Additional 17492)". *The Modern Language Review*, Vol. 90, No. 2. April 1995.

Howlett, R. "The Household Accounts of Kenninghall Palace in the Year 1525". *Norfolk Archeology*, 15. 1904.

Hutchinson, R. *House of Treason: The Rise and Fall of a Tudor Dynasty.* Orion Books, Ltd., 2009.

The Last Days of Henry VIII: Conspiracy, Treason and Heresy at the Court of the Dying Tyrant. Phoenix, 2006.

I

Ives, E. W. *The Life and Death of Anne Boleyn: The Most Happy.* Blackwell Publishing, 2010.

L

Latymer, W. "William Latymer's Cronickille of Anne Bulleyne". Ed. Maria Dowling, *Camden Miscellany*, xxx. Camden Soc. 4th ser. 39. 1990.

Letters and Papers, Foreign and Domestic, of the Reign of Henry VIII. 28 Volumes. Ed. Brewer, J.S. & Gairdner, J. Institute of Historical Research (1862-1932).

Lipscomb, S. *1536: The Year that Changed Henry VIII.* Lion Hudson, 2009.

Lovell, M.S. *Bess of Hardwick: First Lady of Chatsworth.* Abacus, 2005.

M

Maclean, J. *The Life of Sir Thomas Seymour.* John Camden Hotten, 1869.

Madden, F. *Privy Purse Expenses of the Princess Mary.* William Pickering, 1831.

Marshall, R.K. *Queen Mary's Women: Female Friends, Family, Servants and Enemies of Mary, Queen of Scots.* John Donald, 2006.

Meline, J.F. *Mary, Queen of Scots, and Her Latest English Historian.* Hurd and Houghton, 1872.

Morgan, R.B. *Reading in English Social History.* Cambridge University Press, 1923.

Murphy, B. *Bastard Prince: Henry VIII's Lost Son.* The History Press, 2014. Kindle edition.

N

Nichols, J.G. *Inventories of the Wardrobe, Plate, Chapel Stuff, Etc. of Henry Fitzroy, Duke of Richmond*. The Camden Society, 1855.

"Mary Richmond, Female Biographies of English History, IV". *Gentleman's Magazine.* May 1845.

Nicolas, N.H. *Privy Purse Expenses of King Henry VIII*. William Pickering, 1827.

Norton, E. *Bessie Blount: Mistress to Henry VIII*. Amberley Publishing, 2012.

The Boleyn Women: The Tudor Femmes Fatales Who Changed English History. Amberley Publishing, 2013.

P

Perry, M. *Sisters to the King*. Andre Deutsch, 2002.

Pole, R. *Pole's Defense of the Unity of the Church*. Newman Press, 1965.

R

Remley, P.G. "Mary Shelton and her Tudor Literary Milieu." Ed. Herman, P.C. *Rethinking the Henrician Era*. Illinois, 1994.

S

Sander, N. *Rise and Growth of the Anglican Schism*. Burns and Oates, 1877.

Schutte, K. *A Biography of Margaret Douglas, Countess of Lennox, (1515-1578): Niece of Henry VIII and Mother-In-Law of Mary, Queen of Scots*. Edwin Mellen, 2002.

Sharp Hume, M.A. *Chronicle of King Henry VIII of England*. George Bell and Sons, 1889.

Shulman, N. *Graven With Diamonds: The Many Lives of Thomas Wyatt*. Short Books, 2012.

St Clare Byrne, M. *The Lisle Letters, Six Volumes*. The University of Chicago Press, 1981.

Steen, S.J. *The Letters of Lady Arbella Stuart*. Oxford University Press, 1994.

Strickland, A. *Lives of the Queens of Scotland and English Princesses Connected with the Regal Succession of Great Britain, Volume 2*. William Blackwood and Sons, 1851.

Strype, J. *Memorials of the Most Reverend Father in God Thomas Cranmer, Volume 1*. Ecclesiastical History Society, 1848.

T

Tremlett, G. *Catherine of Aragon: Henry's Spanish Queen*. Faber & Faber, 2010.

W

Warnicke, R.M. *Women of the English Renaissance and Reformation*. Greenwood Press, 1983.

Weir, A. *Mary Boleyn: 'The Great and Infamous Whore'*. Vintage, 2011.

The Lady in the Tower: The Fall of Anne Boleyn. Vintage, 2010.

Whitelock, A. *Elizabeth's Bedfellows: An Intimate History of the Queen's Court*. Bloomsbury Publishing, Plc., 2013.

Wriothesley, C. *A Chronicle of England During the Reigns of the Tudors, from A.D. 1485 to 1559*. Camden Society, 1875.

Made in the USA
Lexington, KY
09 December 2015